THE PONTIFICAL DECREES

AGAINST THE

𝕯octrine of the 𝕮arth's 𝕸ovement,

AND THE

ULTRAMONTANE DEFENCE OF THEM.

BY THE

REV. WILLIAM W. ROBERTS.

ἡ ἀλήθεια ἐλευθερώσει ὑμᾶς.—Ιωαν. viii. 32.

Parker and Co.

OXFORD, AND 6 SOUTHAMPTON STREET,
STRAND, LONDON.

1885.

24. e. 100.

In rebus obscuris atque a nostris oculis remotissimis, si qua inde scripta etiam divina legerimus quæ possint salva fide qua imbuimur, alias atque alias parere sententias; in nullam earum nos præcipiti affirmatione ita projiciamus, ut si forte diligentius discussa veritas eam recte labefactaverit, corruamus.—S. Aug. *De Gen. ad Lit.* lib. i. c. xviii. 37.

INTRODUCTION.

I CANNOT republish my essay of 1870 and not notice Dr. Ward's rejoinder. And the apology I have to offer for doing both these things is that the explanation of the case my critic defended against me has recently been adopted in a work that is likely to hold a high place in Roman Catholic literature. I refer to the admirable *Catholic Dictionary*, by Father Addis and Mr. Thomas Arnold. When so accomplished and honest a writer as the last-named gentleman can think that his article on "Galileo" adequately represents the anti-Roman argument supplied by the facts narrated, and that Dr. Ward's answer is satisfactory, such a reconsideration of the subject as the following pages may promote can hardly be deprecated as uncalled for and out of date. Taking, then, my essay as read, I will at once deal with Dr. Ward's remarks on it. They will be found in two articles of the *Dublin Review* of the year 1871, entitled respectively "Copernicanism and Pope Paul V.," and "Galileo and the Pontifical Congregations."

I object in limine to my opponent's account of one of the main points at issue. "This pamphlet," he observes, "is directed to the establishment of two principal conclusions: firstly, that Paul V. condemned heliocentricism ex cathedrâ; and secondly, that even were the case otherwise, the Roman Congregations so acted in the matter of Galileo as to show themselves utterly unworthy of that intellectual submission which has been claimed as due to them by Pius IX., speaking ex cathedrâ."

I recognise as mine this second conclusion,* but assur-

---

* *I.e.* as against those who hold that the Günther Brief, the Munich Brief, and the Syllabus are certainly ex cathedrâ utterances.

edly not the first, in the sense my opponent would hold
me responsible for it; for in the next page he would make
me mean that " Paul V. defined it to be a dogma of the
Faith that the sun moves ·round the earth precisely as
Pius IX. long afterwards defined it to be a dogma of the
Faith that Mary was immaculately conceived." Had my
thesis been this, my opponent's expressions of surprise
at my supposing it arguable would be most natural.
When the doctrine of the Immaculate Conception was
defined, all the conditions of an ex cathedrâ Act were
so abundantly and clearly fulfilled that no Roman Catholic
theologian would be permitted to raise a doubt on the
subject. I do not for a moment pretend that heliocentricism was condemned by any judgment of which the same
may be said; neither have I attempted to prove that it
was. My contention was a very different one; and I will
try to explain and vindicate it.

I found it laid down by such distinguished repre-
sentatives of the Ultramontane school as Cardenas, La
Croix, Zaccaria, and Bouix, that Congregational decrees,
confirmed by the Pope and published by his express
order, emanate from the Pontiff in his capacity of Head
of the Church, and are ex cathedrâ in such sense as to
make it infallibly certain that doctrines so propounded
as true, are true. This, according to D. Bouix, is the
opinion to be held. The contrary, though not condemned, is, he says, "futilis et certo falsa." Moreover, it seemed to me, as it did to Dr. Ward, that this
opinion was powerfully supported by certain utterances
and Acts of the Holy See itself. Take, for instance, the
language I quoted in my pamphlet, used by Pius IX. in
the Brief *Eximiam tuam*, in reference to the original decree
prohibiting Günther's works. That decree was a simple
edict of the Index, having the usual notice that the Pope
had ratified the decision and ordered its publication. Yet
the Pope speaks of it as having been approved "by his
supreme authority;" and remarks that, "sanctioned by our
authority and published by our order, it plainly ought
to have sufficed that the whole question should be judged

finally decided—*penitus dirempta*, and that all who boast
of the Catholic profession should clearly and distinctly
understand .... that the doctrine contained in Günther's
books could not be considered sound," "sinceram haberi
non posse doctrinam Güntherianis libris contentam."
How, in the name of common sense, could a decree possibly erroneous have made it clear to all Catholics that
the doctrine of the books thereby prohibited could not
be sound? And how could such a decree have plainly
sufficed to determine the whole question at issue?

A still more striking case in point is afforded by the
history of the decrees condemnatory of Louvain traditionalism. Two accounts of what happened, the one in
a measure supplementing the other, together with the
authoritative documents cited, will be found in the first
volume of the *Dublin Review* for 1868. From these it
appears that, in June 1843, Professor Ubaghs, of the University of Louvain, received notice that the Congregation
of the Index had decreed that his works on *Theodicea* and
Logic contained errors he would be required to correct in
a future edition. The points to which his attention was
directed on this occasion were his deliverances touching
the impossibility of demonstrating, in the proper sense of
the term, external metaphysical truths in general, and
God's existence in particular. The professor accordingly
made some changes; but the Congregation was still dis-
satisfied with his language, and passed another decree to
the effect that he had not made the corrections required.
We gather from a later document (Cardinal Patrizi's letter
of Oct. 11, 1864) that both these decrees were confirmed
by Gregory XVI.

After this the contention between the supporters
and opponents of the professor's opinions was allowed
to go on for some years. But the publication, in
1859, of a work by Canon Lupus, entitled *Traditionalism
and Rationalism Examined*, and the judgment of an eminent Roman theologian that no sound Catholic could hold
the opinions on traditionalism taught at Louvain, drove
four of the professors to send an exposition of their doc-

trine to Cardinal de Andrea, Prefect of the Index, to be submitted to the Congregation. Instead, however, of doing so, the Cardinal contented himself with the judgment of certain theologians, and returned an answer on his own account, wherein he praised the professors for their submission to the Apostolic See, and declared that the doctrine referred to him "is among those that may be freely disputed on either side by Christian philosophers." But his letter, having no authority—for it did not even profess to be from the Congregation—only supplied fresh matter for contention.

In the following year, July 31, 1861, the Belgian Bishops wrote to the Rector of the University of Louvain, with a view to restore peace. The professors engaged to adhere to all the counsels and rules laid down for them. Then the Pope himself interposed with an Apostolical Letter, dated Dec. 19, 1861, in which he utterly disavowed Cardinal de Andrea's letter, as having no authority whatever. He declared that "the definitive examination and judgment of the doctrines in dispute appertained solely to the Apostolic See," "Quarum definitivum examen et judicium ad hanc Apostolicam Sedem unice pertinent." That until the Holy See should definitively pronounce judgment on the matter, neither the advocates nor opponents of the opinions in debate were to say that what they taught was the one, true, and the only admissible doctrine on the subject: "Volumus atque mandamus, ut earumdem doctrinarum tum fautores tum oppugnatores, donec definitivum de ipsis doctrinis judicium hæc Sancta Sedes proferre existimaverit, se omnino abstineant sive docendo . . . . sive factis sive consiliis, aliquam ex prædictis philosophicis ac theologicis doctrinis exhibere ac tueri, veluti unicam, veram, et solam admittendam, ac veluti Catholicæ Universitati propriam." Observe, the Pontiff here plainly asserts that no judgment but a judgment exclusively (unice) of the Holy See ought to be accepted as decisive on the points at issue. He implies, therefore, that the decrees he subsequently required the professors to accept as decisive, were to be recognised as expressive of the judgment exclusively (*unice*) of the Holy See.

The Pope then commissioned the Congregations of the Inquisition and Index to examine the whole matter; and on Oct. 11, 1864, Cardinal Patrizi wrote to the Belgian Bishops, announcing the result. The united Congregations resolved that Professor Ubaghs had not really corrected the errors censured in 1843 and 1844. They, therefore, commanded him to do so. They further said that they must not be understood to approve certain other opinions advocated in the more recent editions of the professor's works. His Holiness Pope Pius IX., it was added, has ratified and confirmed with his authority this their sentence.

Professor Ubaghs again set himself to prepare a fresh edition of his works, and in 1865 placed copies of it in the hands of the Roman authorities, intending to publish should his corrections be approved. But the judgment he elicited on this occasion was even more unfavourable to him than that of 1864. The Congregations ruled that the new edition still contained, in substance, the errors previously noted; and they added that they observed in the professor's works teachings very similar to some of the seven propositions condemned by the Holy Office in Sept. 1861; and other opinions were there to be found, at least incautiously expressed, concerning traducianism and the vital principle in man. The two Congregations, therefore, pronounced judgment, "That in the philosophical works hitherto published by G. C. Ubaghs, and especially in his *Logic* and *Theodicea*, doctrines or opinions are found that cannot be taught without danger," "quæ absque periculo tradi non possunt;" "and this judgment our Holy Lord Pope Pius IX. has ratified and confirmed by his supreme authority." "Quare Eminentissimi Cardinales in hanc devenere sententiam:—In libris philosophicis a G. C. Ubaghs hactenus in lucem editis, et præsertim *Logica* et *Theodicea* inveniri doctrinas seu opiniones, quæ absque periculo tradi non possunt. Quam sententiam SSmus. D. N. Pius Papa IX. ratam habuit et suprema sua

auctoritate confirmavit." The decree was notified in a
letter from Cardinal Patrizi dated March 2, 1866. The
writer added :—There is no doubt that Professor Ubaghs,
considering his great virtue, and the other professors of
Louvain that hold the same opinions, will obey this decision. And the Archbishop is commanded, in the Pope's
name, to take measures with his suffragans to give effect
to the resolutions notified.

On the receipt of this decree the Belgian Bishops sent
a letter, dated March 21, to the Rector and Professors of
Louvain, to which they all replied, and gladly gave a
declaration of "filial obedience, to be laid at the feet of his
Holiness." Professor Ubaghs resigned his chair, and set
himself to correct his works; and from this time his name
is no more mentioned in connection with these trans-
actions.

"But still," we read, "some difficulty arose with regard
to the interpretation of the last decree. Some said that
it was disciplinary, not doctrinal. We must not *teach* the
condemned opinion"—such was their language—"but we
may *preserve it in our heart*." Others considered that the
exposition of doctrine drawn up by the four professors
in 1860 was not touched by this decision. M. Laforêt
deemed this last opinion probable and lawful, and so did
Professor Beelen; and Professor Lefebre wrote to the
same effect to the Bishop of Namur, who, in conjunction
with two other Bishops, sent the letter to the Holy See.
The Cardinal of Malines also communicated to Cardinal
Patrizi his knowledge of the doubts about the force of
the decree. The latter, in his reply, requested the Archbishop to convene a meeting of the Bishops to take
measures to secure a full, perfect, and absolute submission of those professors who adhered to the opinions censured, to the decision of the Holy See: "Fac igitur quæso
ut Episcopi suffraganei tui quam primum apud te con-
veniant, hac de re agant et efficiant ut professores notatis
opinionibus jam adhærentes resolutioni S. Sedis plene,
perfecte, absoluteque, se submittant."

In obedience to this letter the Bishops met at the

end of July, and invited MM. Beelen and Lefebre to
express their sentiments. This they did at length,
affirming at the same time that they most heartily
embraced all the decisions of the Holy See, but that
it was not evident to them, from the letters of March 2nd
and June 3rd, that any decision had condemned the
exposition of doctrine they had forwarded to Cardinal
de Andrea. They then, at the request of the Bishops,
drew up a carefully worded statement of their opinions
to be submitted to Rome, ending with a request to be
informed by the Apostolic See whether it has condemned
such tenets theologically considered, and whether, therefore, they must be entirely rejected by every Catholic :—

"Per gratum nobis erit a Sede Apostolica edoceri,
utrum ea, quæ hic a nobis sunt exposita, ab ipsa theo-
logice fuerint damnata, ideoque a quovis catholico prorsus
sint rejicienda."

In forwarding this to Rome, the Bishops added a
letter of their own to the Pope, dated August 1st, 1866,
giving an account of the doubts that prevailed touching
the scope and force of the decrees, and they earnestly
begged the Pontiff to say whether the doctrine of the
professors was really reprobated in those decrees.

Cardinal Patrizi, on the 30th of the same month,
replied in the Pope's name. He remarked that it was
wonderful how such doubts could be entertained; that of
course the exposition of February 1860 had been fully
taken into account. "Assuredly," he said, "it is the duty
of Catholics, and still more so of ecclesiastics, to subject
themselves to the decrees of the Holy See, fully, perfectly,
and absolutely, and to put away contentions that would
interfere with the sincerity of their assent." "Porro viri
catholici, multo vero magis ecclesiastici id muneris
habent, ut decretis S. Sedis, plene, perfecte, absoluteque
se subjiciant, e medio sublatis contentionibus, quæ sin-
ceritati assensus officerent." "I write these things in
the name of the Holy Father, that you may make them
known to the Bishops your suffragans, and that both you
and they may admonish in the Lord, and more and more

exhort the above-named professors and those who think with them to acquiesce *ex animo*, as it becomes them, in the judgment of the Apostolic See," "ut sententiæ Apostolicæ Sedis ex animo, sicut eos decet, acquiescant."

On this the Bishops drew up the following formula of submission, to be signed by all the professors that had in any way committed themselves to the opinions noted:—

"In compliance with your orders I hasten to offer you this written testimony of my filial obedience, and I most humbly entreat you to lay it at the feet of our Most Holy Father Pope Pius IX. I fully, perfectly, and absolutely submit myself to the decisions of the Apostolic See issued on the 2nd of March and the 30th of August of this year, and I acquiesce in them *ex animo*. And, therefore, from my heart I reprobate and reject all doctrine opposed thereto, and in particular the exposition of doctrine that was subscribed to by four professors, and sent on the 1st of February 1860 to his Eminence the Cardinal Prefect of the Sacred Congregation of the Index, and other opinions touching the questions mooted at Louvain that the Apostolic See has reprobated."

" Obsequens mandatis vestris hocce documentum filialis obedientiæ vobis exhibere festino, humillime rogans, ut per manus vestras ad pedes SSmi Domini Pii P.P. IX. deponatur.

"Decisionibus S. Sedis Apostolicæ diei 2 Martii et 30 Augusti hujus anni plene, perfecte, absoluteque me subjicio, et ex animo acquiesco. Ideoque ex corde reprobo et rejicio quamcunque doctrinam oppositam, nominatim expositionem doctrinæ a quatuor professoribus subscriptam et die 1 Februarii anno 1860 ad Emum. Cardinalem Præfectum S. Congregationis Indicis transmisam, aliaque ad quæstionem Lovanii agitatam spectantia, quæ Sedes Apostolica reprobavit.

" Profunda veneratione et omnimoda subjectione permaneo,

"Eminentissime Princeps, Illmi. et Rmi. Antistites.

" Humillimus et obedientissimus famulus.

" Lovanii, Dec. 1866."

Is not this as complete an act of submission as was ever exacted to any ex cathedrâ decision that was not a definition of faith? Compare it, *e.g.*, with the submission certain professors were required to yield to Pope Gregory's Brief that condemned the errors of Hermes—a judgment undoubtedly ex cathedrâ. (See *Dublin Review*, January 1868, p. 233.)

If, as Cardinal Franzelin seems to teach,[*] the assent *of faith* is claimed in the case of every ex cathedrâ utterance, the Pope has long ago implicitly defined the doctrine of his infallibility in minor censures, and to deny that doctrine would unquestionably be against the faith, and constructive heresy. But this it confessedly is not. In the Bull "Apostolicæ Sedis moderationi," teachers and defenders of propositions condemned by the Holy See, "sub excommunicationis pœna latæ sententiæ," are placed in a separate class from offenders against the faith; and they incur excommunication less strictly reserved even than those who read, without license, a book condemned in an Apostolic Letter.

No one refused to sign the formula, and it looked as if traditionalism at Louvain had received its death-blow. For the circumstances under which it once more put forth a feeler, we must turn to the April number of the *Dublin Review* for 1871. The last chapter of this remarkable history is even more significant for my purpose than the preceding.

It appears that, though the Vatican Council condemned traditionalism in the "Dei Filius," it did not specially mention that modified form of it that had been advocated at Louvain. The omission was welcomed by some as an indication that the doctrines so heartily and thoroughly reprobated four years ago might once more be professed. Rome was sounded on the subject, and Cardinal Patrizi, at the command of Pius IX., sent the following response, dated August 7, 1870: "That by the said Synodal Constitution (the 'Dei Filius'), especially by the monitum at its conclusion, all the decrees of the two Con-

---

[*] *De Divina Traditione et Scriptura*, pp. 124, 139.

gregations issued on the matter, and especially the one contained in the letters I sent to the Belgian Bishops on March 2, 1866, have not only not been annulled nor weakened, but, on the contrary, have been strengthened by a new sanction." The *monitum* cited is this : "Since it is not sufficient to shun heretical pravity, unless those errors also be diligently avoided which more or less nearly approach it, we admonish all men of the further duty of observing those constitutions and decrees by which such erroneous opinions as are not here specifically enumerated have been proscribed and condemned by the Holy See."

The *Civilta* of March 18 (p. 721) declares that the Pope's reply is more useful than any *treatise* "for the purpose of clearing up better a special point concerning the extension of the object and the Acts of the (Pope's) Apostolic Magisterium." And the *Dublin Review* adds : "The Holy Father's response declares in effect that the Congregational decrees of 1867, expressing as they did the Pope's confirmation, are to be accounted Pontifical ex cathedrâ Acts."

This much is clear :—According to the mind of Rome, expressed in the declarations and acts we have considered, judgments of the class in question are to be accounted, in a very proper sense, decrees of the Holy See; the doctrine they propound ought to be accepted by all Catholics with unreserved assent—"plene, perfecte, absoluteque ;" and, lastly, according to the response of Pius IX., they are decrees of the Holy See in the sense intended by a General Council, referring to such decisions under circumstances that almost preclude the notion that any but infallibly true judgments could have been meant.

Such being the case, how can the Ultramontanist meet the mistake that Rome made in condemning heliocentricism ? For was not the judgment in the matter confirmed by the Pope and published by his special order ? Had it not, therefore, the same security against error that the Günther and Louvain decrees had ? No, it was said, there was a most noteworthy difference. Granting that the anti-Copernican decree must have been sanctioned by the Pope, and that it could not have been issued without his order; granting that it simply published, as Bellarmine's certificate declares it did, the Pope's own judgment on the matter—owing to an accident, or, as we prefer to say, owing to an express interposition of Providence in favour of our doctrine, the part the Pontiff took in the matter was not officially notified, as it should have been, to the Church, and in consequence of this omission the decree has no title to be ranked with those under comparison. For a decree must be estimated exclusively by the marks of authority it exhibits to the Church. All that went on behind the scenes, if not officially notified, must be ignored and discounted. The anti-Copernican decree, *as it came before the faithful*, was a mere Congregational edict, presumably indeed issued under the Pope's order, but carrying with it no official guarantee whatever that his Holiness had given it his special approval, or intended it to be regarded as invested with his supreme authority. In other words, the judgment was a confessedly fallible utterance, of a kind that no Ultramontane theologian in the world would have the slightest difficulty in admitting might be erroneous.

Such in substance was the answer; but it is demonstrably indefensible. As I pointed out, the absence of the clause, on which so much stress is laid, is to be accounted for, neither by accident, nor by a special Providence in favour of Ultramontane opinions, but by the simple circumstance that the practice of affixing such notices to Congregational decrees is, comparatively speaking, a recent one, and was not observed in the case of any decree until many years after Galileo's time.

Apart from other arguments, the very history of the Louvain controversy that we have been considering, supplies proof that the Pope may exercise his supreme authority in decisions that he does not notify, and does not intend should be notified, to the Church at large. For, according to the writer in the April number of the *Dublin Review* (p. 576), the decrees that the Pope had confirmed by his supreme authority, and to which the professors were required to yield such complete submission, had not been, and have not, even to this day, been officially published by the Holy See. " It should be borne in mind," he says, "that the decrees of 1843-4 were not published for twenty years, and that both they and the later decrees of 1864 and 1866 were ultimately made public, *contrary to the wishes and without the authorisation of the Holy See, which had required that they should be kept secret.*" But what must, on its own principle, be simply fatal to the answer, is the fact it completely ignores, that although the anti-Copernican decrees were issued in 1616 without the clause, they were reissued in 1664 with a far more significant and authoritative guarantee of Papal approval than any number of clauses.

Whatever authority a decision can be supposed to possess in virtue of a notice from the secretary of a Congregation that the Pope has ratified it, and ordered its publication, it must possess far more indisputably in virtue of an assurance to the same effect given by the Pope himself in a Bull addressed to the Universal Church. I say far more indisputably, for it might be urged, on the ground taken in the answer, that the clause is not a Papal Act, that it tells us only what the Pope did behind the scenes; but the Bull " Speculatores " was itself a Papal Act of supreme authority; and by that Act the Pontiff publicly, in the face of the whole Church, confirmed and approved the decrees with his Apostolic authority, and made himself responsible for their publication, declaring that the Index to which they had been attached by his order was to be accounted as inserted in the Bull itself.

I conclude, then, that if all Catholics ought to have inferred, from the Pope's confirmation by his supreme authority of the Günther decree, that it was infallibly certain that that philosopher's prohibited opinions could not be sound; if the Louvain professors were bound in conscience to recognise in the decisions that condemned their tenets the judgment exclusively—*unice*—of the Holy See; à *fortiori* all Catholics ought to have concluded from the Bull " Speculatores " and the decrees of Paul V. and

Urban VIII. that it was infallibly certain that heliocentricism was false. And I submit that this conclusion remains untouched by any argument Dr. Ward, or any one else, has advanced. But to say this is not to say that Paul V. or any other Pope "defined it to be a dogma of the faith that the sun moves round the earth, precisely as Pius IX. defined it to be a dogma of the faith that Mary was immaculately conceived."

Nor can the difficulty I suggest be got rid of by adopting Cardinal Franzelin's* modification of D. Bouix's opinion. For although the Cardinal does not regard the judgments in question as ex cathedrâ, in the sense of being infallibly true, he is forced, considering the kind and degree of authority claimed for them by the Holy See, to maintain that they are infallibly safe—safe, meaning by the term not merely that those who yield them the assent demanded may do so without risk of being called to account for their act, but safe, in the sense that it is infallibly certain that the doctrine propounded may be embraced by all Catholics with full interior assent, without peril to the cause of the faith, or to the interests of religion.† But it is almost as easy to show that the condemnation of Copernicanism was not in this sense a safe judgment, as to show that it was not a true one; to prove that it was a dangerous mistake, as to prove that it was a mistake at all. For what was the doctrine of that judgment as it was authoritatively interpreted by Rome? This:—That heliocentricism is false, and altogether contrary to the divine Scriptures, meaning by the phrase, as the monitum of 1620 explained it, "repugnant to the true and Catholic interpretation of Scripture." In other words, according to the ruling of Urban VIII. and the Pontifical Congregation of the Inquisition, the decision taught that

---

* *De Divina Traditione et Scriptura*, pp. 127-9.

† " In hujusmodi declarationibus licet non sit doctrinæ *veritas infallibilis*, quia hanc decidendi ex hypothesi non est intentio; *est tamen infallibilis securitas*. Securitatem dico tum *objectivam doctrinæ declaratæ* (vel simpliciter vel pro talibus adjunctis), tum subjectivam quatenus omnibus tutum est eam amplecti, et tutum non est nec absque violatione debitæ submissionis erga magisterium divinitus constitutum fieri potest, ut eam amplecti recusent " (p. 127).

heliocentricism is a heresy to be abjured, cursed, and detested with the other heresies opposed to the Holy Catholic and Apostolic Roman Church.

Now, it is as clear as daylight that if all Catholics had embraced this doctrine with unreserved assent, "plene, perfecte, et absolute," all Catholics would have held it to be of faith that heliocentricism is false, and thus the whole Church would so far have been in error in its faith. But for the whole Church to be in error in any point it holds to be of faith is plainly irreconcilable with the passive infallibility claimed for it by theologians,* or even with its claims to be infallible in its ordinary magisterium, for what it believes it will surely teach—"credidi propter quod locutus sum." And apart from this consideration, obviously it must be against the cause of the Christian faith for all Christians to be persuaded that its teachings conflict with, and demand the suppression and complete elimination from thought of, opinions that are on their way to be proved true.

Again, the decision peremptorily claimed the authority of Holy Scripture for a doubtful theory, a theory some of the ablest scientific men of the age thought would probably be proved false. It therefore risked bringing into discredit what it was the Church's duty to do her utmost to protect. It was, therefore, a rash decision.

Moreover, if, as Rome teaches, it is of great moment in the interests of religion that Catholic men of science should humbly yield assent to the decisions of Pontifical Congregations, whatever tends to destroy confidence in such decisions must, from her point of view, be detri-

---

* Thus Bellarmine (De Eccles. lib. iii. c. 14, art. 3) : "Ecclesia non potest errare, id est, id quod tenent omnes fideles tanquam de fide, necessario est verum et de fide, et similiter id quod docent omnes Episcopi tanquam ad fidem pertinens, necessario est verum et de fide." And Suarez (De Fide, disp. v. sec. 6) : "Ecclesia non potest errare in iis quæ credit certa de fide, etiam per invincibilem ignorantiam ; id quoque videtur esse de fide, quia si per ignorantiam invincibilem errare potest, tota ejus fides esset dubia, in singulis posset dubitari an non per ignorantiam erraret, quod non potest dici de Ecclesia quæ est ' columna et firmamentum veritatis' (1 Tim. iii. 15), et cui a Christo ejus capite et sponso promissa est infallibilis Spiritus Sancti assistentia: ' Cum venerit Paracletus docebit vos omnem veritatem ' (Joan. xvi. 13)."

mental to those interests. But how can the man of science not distrust those who, in return for loving obedience, have given him not true but false guidance?

"The Pope and the Cardinals," remarks Mr. Arnold,[*] "believed, in 1616, that if every one might freely teach at universities or by printed books that the earth revolved round the sun, a great weakness of religious faith would ensue, owing to the apparent inconsistency of such teaching with a number of well-known passages in the Bible." No one at any time could reasonably believe that the doctrine of the earth's revolution round the sun would weaken the religious faith of persons holding the opinion that the inconsistency is only apparent, and not real; and it was precisely the advocacy of *this opinion*—the opinion of F. Foscarinus—" that the doctrine of the earth's motion is in harmony with the truth, and *is not opposed to Holy Scripture*," that the decision of 1616 prohibited and condemned, "lest an opinion of this kind should spread to the destruction of Catholic truth." And when the time should come that every one must be taught at universities and by printed books, whether the Pope and the Cardinals wished it or not, that the earth revolves round the sun, whose faith would be likely to suffer then? Would it not be the faith of those who, by looking to Popes and Cardinals for what to believe, and by yielding unreserved assent to the decisions of Pontifical Congregations had learnt to believe that the doctrine of the earth's motion contradicts, not merely the apparent meaning of certain passages in the Bible, but *Scripture, and its true and Catholic interpretation?*

Nor can a Roman Catholic say with Dr. Ward that the mistake inculcated " neither contradicts revealed truth nor leads by legitimate consequence to such contradiction." For to hold that any part of Scripture, in its true and Catholic interpretation, or in the only sense its language will, properly speaking, bear, teaches what is false, leads, as I shall show, to an implicit denial of the Vatican dogma, that the whole of Scripture has been

* *Catholic Dictionary*, p. 865.

B

written by inspiration of the Holy Ghost, and has God for
its author.

It is clear, therefore, that the doctrine of the anti-
Copernican decrees was not less unsafe than it was untrue. *

In some cases, though not in this, a controversialist
may find Cardinal Franzelin's opinion useful, but in point
of consistency with admitted principles and intrinsic reasonableness it contrasts most unfavourably with the older
view. If the gift of truth and never-failing faith has
been bestowed on the Holy See, that the faithful may be
sure of getting a supply of heavenly food unadulterated
with human error, the presumption is enormously strong
that God will not permit the Pope to use his supreme
authority to impose on the mind of the Church doctrines
that are false, in the sense in which they profess to be
true ; and still more incredible is it that He will permit
such an abuse of power when the doctrine has to do with
what is matter of faith. And the proposition that all
Catholics, even those well qualified to form a judgment
on the subject, are bound in conscience to abandon what
they hold to be true, and embrace with unreserved assent
what they hold to be false, at the bidding of a body of
men who do not even profess to be divinely secured from
error, whose office did not protect their predecessors from
making egregious blunders, who avowedly may be in
error on the very point in question, who are not necessarily wiser, more learned, more unprejudiced, than those
whose submission they claim, is scarcely recommended to

---

* When the object is purity of doctrine an erroneous decision cannot but
be harmful. The Church is not supposed to interfere in matters of no
moment, and some of the instances cited of safe but possibly untrue judgments were on matters of great importance. Moreover, as Dr. Ward (*Dublin
Review*, July 1874, p. 25) observes, "No one can tell what future harm
might ensue from a mistaken doctrine, however at the time comparatively
harmless." Cardinal Franzelin's remark (op. cit. p. 127)—"Non coinci-
dere hæc duo, infallibilem veritatem et securitatem, manifestum est vel ex
eo, quod secus nulla doctrina probabilis aut probabilior posset dici sana et
secura"—simply involves the point at issue in a cloud of confusion. The
question is not whether an opinion that is only probable, may not frequently
be a safe ground of action, nor whether an opinion that is only probable, may
not be safely held as probable. Of course it may. But whether, when the
object is the formation of convictions exclusively true, propositions that are
possibly false can be safely embraced by the intellect as certainly true.

the reason, because the authority of those men is called
sacred, and the assent they claim religious. The interests
of truth are also sacred; and disloyalty to those interests, an unreal humility, a make-believe that there is no
room for doubt, when there is, can be no acceptable
homage to Him, who is the Truth Itself, and who desires
to be worshipped "in spirit and in truth."

Dr. Ward's main argument against the first part of
my pamphlet is reducible to the following: If the decision
of 1616 was infallibly true, it was ex cathedrâ; if it was
ex cathedrâ, from the nature of the censure, it was a
definition of faith; if it was a definition of faith, it propounded the doctrine of the sun's diurnal movement as
a dogma, precisely as the Bull "Ineffabilis" propounded
as a dogma the doctrine of the Blessed Virgin's Immaculate Conception; but it is simply absurd to suppose that
the Pope would propound a dogma of the faith in the
form of a Congregational decree, therefore the original
supposition is absurd—*a monstrum nulla ratione redemptum.*

"It is," he remarked (p. 352), "essential to the present
inquiry that all our readers should understand *how much*
is implied in the allegations of this pamphlet. Any one
who reads the facts therein so usefully brought together
will see that the charge against heliocentricism was nothing
less than a charge of *heresy.* It was considered by the
Pope and the ecclesiastical authorities that this theory is
'opposed to Scripture' (p. 5); 'contrary to Scripture'
(p. 20); 'repugnant to Scripture' (p. 21); 'a heresy'
(p. 21). Supposing, therefore, that Paul V. had really
pronounced this judgment ex cathedrâ, his declaration
would have been nothing less than a definition of faith.
In other words, according to our opponent, Paul .V.
defined it to be a dogma of the faith that the sun moves
round the earth, precisely as Pius IX. long afterwards
defined it to be a dogma of the faith that Mary was
immaculately conceived."

It is satisfactory to obtain so frank an acknowledg-
ment from my opponent that the terms of the condemnation meant "heresy," and nothing short of it; that the
Pope and the ecclesiastical authorities considered, and

in effect said, that heliocentricism is a heresy. Now, I
submit that, no matter who says it, whether a Pope
speaking ex cathedrâ, or a mere layman, whoever says
categorically that an opinion is "heresy," *ipso facto* says
that the contradictory of that opinion has been revealed
by God with sufficient certainty to oblige a Catholic to
accept it by an act of divine faith.   To generate an obligation of faith, it is by no means necessary that the witness
to the fact of revelation should claim for his testimony
infallible certainty, but only such certainty as will exclude
all prudent fear, *ne non locutus sit Deus*.   And to say that
an opinion is "heresy" is to say more than that its contradictory is matter of faith.   There is an implicit reference
to the infallible testimony of the Church.   The assertion
means that the contradictory is not only of faith, but of
Catholic faith.* And De Lugo remarks that this holds good
whenever an opinion can be properly called "heresy,"
simply because of its repugnancy to Scripture. "Ego. . . .
puto, in casu proposito, si constat sufficienter de revelatione Dei in Scriptura contenta, constare etiam sufficienter
de propositione Ecclesiæ, atque adeo non posse dissensum
excusari ab heresi ex defectu solum propositionis, seu
applicationis ab Ecclesia faciendæ, quare si dissensus sit
error contra fidem, quia constat sufficienter de revelatione
Dei, erit etiam contra propositionem Ecclesiæ, *quia eodem
modo constat de propositione Ecclesiæ.   Nam Ecclesia clare
et manifeste proponit credendam Scripturam, et omnia et
singula in ea contenta ; si ergo manifeste constat, aliquid in
Scriptura contineri, æque manifeste constare debet id ab
Ecclesia nobis credendum proponi*. . . . Si communiter in
Ecclesia dubitetur, vel saltem non habeatur pro certo et
indubitato, licet aliqui eum (sensum) manifeste percipiant,
ita ut prudenter formidare non possint, et ideo dissentiendo
peccant graviter contra fidem, non tamen credo eos esse
proprie et stricte hæreticos. Ratio autem est, quia hæresis,
ut sæpe diximus est secta seu divisio, et hæreticus est

---

* "Dicere," says De Lugo, " de objecto quod est hæresis, est dicere quod
sit objectum contradicens objecto a Deo revelato, et sufficienter ab Ecclesia
proposito, atque ideo aptum ut terminet hæresim formalem in illud affirm-
ante nisi ignorantia, vel aliquid aliud excusat" (*De Virtute Div. Fidei*,
disp. xx. § 1).

sectarius, quia secat et dividit unitatem Ecclesiæ, seque a reliquo Ecclesiæ corpore et sensu dividit, sectándo, et amplectendo proprium sensum et opinionem, contra id quod Ecclesia sentit " (*De Virt. Div. Fidei*, disp. xx. sect. ii. 58, 59).

If, then, the Pope said in effect that heliocentricism was a heresy, he said in effect that it was not only *de fide*, but *de fide Catholicâ*, that it was false ; that it was not only *de fide*, but *de fide Catholicâ*, that its contradictory was true. In what capacity he spoke, and whether he meant what he said, are further questions, but it is a great point to have it conceded that he did in effect declare heliocentricism to be a " heresy." But we also learn from the statement of a Pontifical Congregation that the utterance was a definition, *i.e.* a final authoritative judgment. We are brought, therefore, to the conclusion that the Pope did in fact publish, through the Congregation of the Index, a definition of faith. Now, suppose for a moment that he did so ex cathedrâ, would it follow that the definition was of the same kind as that by which Pius IX. decided the question of the Immaculate Conception ? And ought it to have been promulgated with like emphasis and solemnity ? Assuredly not. The definition of the Bull "Ineffabilis " was put forward to make that of Catholic faith which confessedly was not so before. Up to the 8th of December 1854 it was, by the force of Bulls that had not been formally revoked, excommunication to call the denial of the doctrine of the Immaculate Conception heresy, or even, if I mistake not, to say that those who impugned it were guilty of grave sin. Since that date, according to the Bull, any one who ventures to think that the doctrine has not been revealed by God, ipso facto, makes shipwreck of his faith, and cuts himself off from the unity of the Church. Clearly the definition was of the nature of a new doctrinal law, and therefore needed a promulgation that would challenge the attention of all Christians. But not every Pontifical definition ex cathedrâ ascribing heresy or repugnancy to Scripture to dissentients is a definition of faith in this sense. By far the greater number are issued, not to generate any

fresh obligation of faith, but to protect and vindicate one
that already exists; and to this class obviously belong ex
cathedrâ censures of books, and propositions, as heretical.
The mode of publishing these judgments will vary of course
with circumstances, but from their nature there is no reason
for their being put forward with any greater emphasis and
solemnity than the evil to be met requires. Why, then,
should they not occasionally be issued through one of the
Congregations the Pope has erected to assist him in dis-
charging his functions as guardian of the faith? And why
should such a mode of publication prejudice their infallibility, if they are certainly Papal decisions, and are known
to be such?

It is important to bear in mind that in the case
before us the Index was called into action to give effect
to the decision of the Congregation of the Holy Office, a
Congregation that is in a very special way under Papal
direction. The Pope as Pope is its president. He is
present at its meetings every Thursday. He has informed the Church that he reserves the presidency of this
Congregation to himself, because of the intimate connection of its decisions with the preservation of the faith.
But if the Pope when he acts as its president never in-
tends to act in the capacity wherein he is divinely secured
from making mistakes, how delusive is this assurance!
What good does the Church get from his presidency?
The Pope not divinely assisted is as likely, nay, in a vast
number of cases, far more likely, to decide erroneously
than some one of his Cardinals. And as to his superior
authority, the more authoritative an erroneous decision is,
the more harm it is likely to do. Either, then, the
judgments in question are ex cathedrâ; or the Pope
claims to decide doctrinal questions for all Catholics in
a capacity in which he is liable to make mistakes, and
so the Holy See may be a source of error to the Church
Universal; or the Pope's prerogative of inerrancy belongs to him even when he is not speaking ex cathedrâ.

Of course there was not, and there could not have
been, the remotest intention of making geocentricism a
matter of faith by the mere force of a definition; but

the question the Copernican controversy raised was
whether the doctrine of the sun's diurnal movement
was not already of faith in virtue of the plain statements of Holy Scripture. The Roman Church, as De
Lugo says, propounds the whole of Holy Scripture, and
every part of it, to be received as the Word of God; so
that to contradict the express assertion of a sacred writer
is not less heresy than to contradict the definition of a
general council. To say that Abraham had not two sons
is not less heresy, than to say that our Lord had not two
wills. Unquestionably the sacred writers, in terms, ascribe
diurnal movement to the sun; therefore, urged the anti-
Copernican theologian, the theory that denies that movement is false and heretical. The conclusion is irresistible,
if the language objected is so express as to forbid the
supposition that not real, but only apparent movement
may be meant. And that it is so express is what
Rome in effect decided, when on the one hand she
pronounced the heliocentric theses false, and altogether
adverse to the divine Scriptures, and on the other condemned as destructive to Catholic truth the advocacy
of an opposite opinion. After this, the thoroughly
submissive Catholic had no alternative but to recognise the heretical character of the new system; yet
the decision plainly proceeded on the assumption that the
matter was not open to legitimate doubt before its issue;
and therefore, however clearly ex cathedrâ, it would
be a judgment of a very different kind from that by
which the doctrine of the Immaculate Conception was
defined.

Dr. Ward's next objection to my thesis is derived from
what he calls the extrinsic circumstances of the decree.

"Let us grant for argument's sake, which certainly
we cannot otherwise grant, that the Pope might possibly have issued a definition of faith in the form of a
Congregational decree which does not so much as
mention his name. In that event, he must have intended
to make manifest by *extrinsic circumstances* what the
decree's intrinsic character rendered so violently improbable. But so far is this from being the case that ex-

trinsic circumstances *taken by themselves* are absolutely decisive against our critic's extraordinary theory. In our former articles we mentioned such facts as the following: 'If one theologian,' we said, 'were more prominent than another in his opposition to Galileo, it was Bellarmine;' yet his words are recorded by F. Grassi, also an opponent of Galileo, to the following effect: 'When a demonstration shall be found to establish the earth's motion, it will be proper to interpret the Holy Scriptures otherwise than they have hitherto been in those passages where mention is made of the movement of the heavens and the stability of the earth.' This was in 1624. Just imagine F. Perrone saying in the year 1862 that some unexpected light may possibly hereafter be obtained, which will make it proper to interpret Scripture and Tradition as opposed to the Immaculate Conception! Yet Bellarmine's statement would be precisely equivalent to this if Copernicanism had really been condemned ex cathedrâ" (*Dublin Review* for April 1871, pp. 355-6).

Observe, the argument is this:—Bellarmine, the distinguished theologian, who took so prominent a part in the proceedings that resulted in the decree of 1616, in 1624—that is, eight years afterwards—used words which show that he did not regard a future demonstration of the truth of Copernicanism as an impossibility; he could not, therefore, have believed that the theory had been condemned by an infallibly true judgment. Obviously, it is essential to Dr. Ward's point, that Bellarmine expressed himself in the sense alleged, *after the question had been decided.* But, so far as I know, there is not a particle of evidence that he did so. Most certainly he did not say anything of the kind at the time Dr. Ward supposed; for in 1624 he had been in his grave nearly four years.* F. Grassi could not have been referring to any recent utterance. The probabilities, almost amounting to a certainty, are, that he was thinking of a remark we find in a letter

---

* It seems that by the time Dr. Ward wrote his July article he had discovered this fact, for in *Galileo and the Pontifical Congregations*, p. 164, we find 1620 quietly fixed on as the true year of Bellarmine's remark. Dr. Ward has given us no authority for so dating it, and I venture to think that he had none to give.

Bellarmine wrote to F. Foscarini in the April of 1615,
i.e. nearly a year before the decision; and thus its irrelevancy
is apparent. Moreover, the words used by no means
necessarily carry with them the implication Dr. Ward
asserts. They are quite consistent with a profound
conviction of the impossibility of the actual occurrence
of the event supposed. And that Bellarmine had this
conviction is indicated by the general import of his
letter, and is attested by other evidence we have of his
mind on the subject.

The Cardinal begins the paragraph immediately preceding the remark in question by observing that the Copernican interpretation of Scripture is already under the ban
of the Council of Trent. "You are aware," he says, "that
the Council forbids us to interpret Scripture in a sense
opposed to the consent of the holy Fathers; and if your
Paternity will read, I do not say only the holy Fathers,
but also modern commentators on Genesis, the Psalms,
Ecclesiastes, Josue, you will find that they all adhere to
the literal exposition that the sun is in the heaven, and
revolves round the earth with very great velocity, and
that the earth is very far from the heaven, and remains
immovable in the centre of the universe. Consider with
yourself, as a man of prudence, whether the Church can
permit Scripture to be interpreted in a sense opposed to
the mind of the holy Fathers, and all modern commentators.* Nor can you reply that the matter is not one of
faith, for though it is not a matter of faith, *ex parte
objecti,* it is a matter of faith, *ex parte dicentis.* Thus the
denier that Abraham had two, and Jacob twelve sons,
would be a heretic, as well as the denier that Christ was
born of a Virgin; for those things, as well as this, the
Holy Ghost has said, speaking through the mouths of
prophets and apostles.

"I say that when it shall be really demonstrated
that the sun is in the centre of the universe, and that
the earth is in the third heaven, and that the sun does

* It is wonderful that Bellarmine did not see that as it never occurred
to the Fathers to doubt the truth of geocentricism, they could not have done
otherwise than interpret Scripture in accordance with that theory.

not go round the earth, but that the earth goes round the sun, then it will be necessary to proceed with great caution in explaining the passages of Scripture that seem to be contradicted, and we must rather say that we do not know what they mean, than say that what has been demonstrated to be true is false. But until it has been shown me, I will not believe in the existence of such a demonstration; for it is by no means the same thing to demonstrate that, granting the sun to be in the centre, and the earth in the third heaven, things would appear as they do now, and to demonstrate that the sun is really in the centre, and the earth in the heaven. The first point I can believe might be demonstrated, but I have the greatest doubt as to the possibility of demonstrating the second; and in a case of doubt we ought not to leave the interpretation of Scripture given by the holy Fathers. I add this consideration,—He who wrote, 'The sun ariseth and setteth, and returneth to his place,' was Solomon, a man who was not only an inspired writer, but one who was divinely endowed beyond all other men with very great wisdom, and learning, and knowledge of the works of nature. It is not likely that he would say anything opposed to what would, or could be proved to be the truth. And if I am told that Solomon is speaking of things as they appear to us, since it seems to us that the sun moves, although it is really the earth that moves, just as when a person leaves the shore, the shore seems to leave the ship; I shall reply that, although to a person leaving the shore it appears as though the shore left him, he is well aware that the case is otherwise, and corrects his erroneous impression by observing that the ship is really in motion, and not the shore; but with regard to the sun and the earth, no one is aware that he has need to correct the error, for all know clearly from experience that the earth stands firm, and that we are not deceived by the eye when we judge that the sun moves,* as also that we are not deceived when we judge that the

* Yet Bellarmine had just said that he could believe that it might be demonstrated that appearances would be the same whether the sun or the earth moved.

moon and the stars move. And let this suffice for the present."*

The writer of this letter holds, (1) that the Copernican interpretation of Scripture is implicitly forbidden by the Council of Trent; (2) that the question at issue is on matter of faith; (3) that although, should it ever be strictly demonstrated that the sun does not move, the fact must be admitted, and Scripture will have to be explained in some way to meet it, yet against the possibility of such a demonstration being found, we must place the express assertion of an inspired writer profoundly versed in natural science that the sun does move, an assertion which we cannot reasonably doubt means that it really moves. The implication is that the truth of Scripture is not compatible with the notion that the supposed demonstration will ever be given.

A few weeks before the date of this letter, the Cardinal's opinion was reported to Galileo, most probably by Prince Cesi, in the following unmistakable terms: "With regard to the opinion of Copernicus, Bellarmine, who heads the Congregations that deal with such matters, told me himself that he holds it to be heretical, and that the doctrine of the earth's motion is *beyond all doubt whatever* (*senza dubbio alcuno*) contrary to Scripture."†

Again, some, if not all, of those twelve theologians that were deputed by the Pope and the Holy Office to qualify the heliocentric propositions, must have been well acquainted with what Bellarmine thought on the matter.

Full time had been allowed for consultation.‡ Previous notice was given of a meeting to be held on February 23rd at the Holy Office, to qualify the propositions. On the 19th of February copies of the propositions were sent to all the Fathers and theologians. It was not until the 24th that the censuring took place. The first proposition, "That the sun is in the centre of the world and altogether immovable by local movement," was unani-

---

* See Appendix A.

† "Quanto all opinione di Copernico, Bellarmino istesso che è de' capi nelle Congregazioni di queste cose, mi ha detto che l' ha per eretica, è che il moto della terra senza dubbio alcuno, e contra la Scrittura " (*Opere de G. G.*, Fl. ed. vol. viii. p. 340). ‡ See Appendix B.

mously declared to be "foolish, philosophically absurd, and formally heretical, inasmuch as it expressly contradicts the declarations of Holy Scripture in many passages, according to the proper meaning of the language used, and the sense in which they have been expounded and understood by the holy Fathers and theologians." The second proposition, " That the earth is not the centre of the world, and moves as a whole, and also with a diurnal movement," was unanimously declared " to deserve the same censure philosophically, and, theologically considered, to be at least erroneous in faith."

Is it credible that censures of this kind would have been pronounced with such unanimity and confidence, in the face of expressed doubts from so distinguished an authority as Bellarmine?

The following account given by Guicciardini of a scene in Consistory shows, at any rate, that it was supposed in Rome at the time, that Bellarmine fully agreed with the Qualifiers, and was influencing the Pope to give public effect to their judgment :* " In Consistory on Wednesday," writes the ambassador, " Cardinal Orsino, it may be with a want of prudence and consideration, spoke to the Pope in favour of Galileo. His Eminence, the Pope said, would do well to persuade Galileo to give up his opinion; and then, somewhat nettled at the Cardinal's reply, his Holiness put a stop to further remark by saying that he had

---

* Von Gebler thinks that this story is discredited by the Vatican ms. and Gherardi's document vi. I cannot see that it is. Guicciardini is writing on Thursday, the 4th of March. The Wednesday he means cannot well be the day before, otherwise he would surely have written " yesterday in Consistory," and he could not have written *jer l' altro* of a meeting that was the result of a conference of the day before. The following, according to the Vatican ms. and Gherardi's documents, was the order of events :—On Wednesday, February 24th, the heliocentric propositions were qualified in virtue of the Pope's order. The following day—Thursday, the day for the Pope to preside at the Congregation of the Holy Office—the censures were reported to the Pope by Cardinal Mellinus, and the Pope gave the two well-known orders, that to Bellarmine, and that to the Commissary of the Holy Office. On Friday, the 26th, these orders were executed, and Galileo submitted ; but the official report of his submission was not made to the Pope until the following Thursday. In the mean time a Congregation must have prepared a draft of the decree we know, from Gherardi's documents, was submitted to the Pope for his approval on the same Thursday, the 4th of March ; and it is not at all improbable that it did so in consequence of instructions received from Bellarmine after his conference with the Pope.

placed the matter in the hands of the Cardinals of the Holy Office. On Orsino's leaving the assembly, the Pope sent for Bellarmine, and talked the matter over with him. The two came to the conclusion that Galileo's opinion is erroneous and heretical, and the day before yesterday, I hear, they caused a Congregation to meet to declare it to be so."*

With regard to Bellarmine's view of the decision itself, all the evidence we have favours the notion that he attributed to it a very high authority. He certainly did not regard it as a simple Congregational judgment. On the contrary, in the certificate he gave Galileo he ascribed it exclusively to the Pope himself, and named the Congregation as the mere medium of its publication.

So much for Dr. Ward's appeal to Bellarmine. His references to Fromond of Louvain, and Riccioli, prove only what I have never denied, that the decree was not one of those judgments, the ex cathedrâ character of which would be regarded as indisputable by all theologians. What they do not prove, what they have not the remotest tendency to prove, is that those who hold that the Papal confirmation of a decree makes it infallibly certain that the doctrine propounded for acceptance is true, or at least safe, in the sense of being calculated to protect the interests of the faith, and not impede the progress of science, can consistently admit that the condemnation of heliocentricism was the mistake we know it was. And if some contemporary theologians were disposed to question the supreme authority of the judgment, I have cited others, and some of them apparently better informed, who pressed it against their Copernically-minded brethren as the voice of the Church herself, as the decision of her supreme Head on earth.†

* Venturi, *Memorie e Lettere*, vol. i. p. 267.
† See also Professor Berti's analysis in his work, *Il Processo Originale di Galileo Galilei*, pp. xci.-xciii., of an unpublished treatise entitled "Vindiciæ Sedis Apostolicæ SS. Tribunalium auctoritate adversus Neo-Pythagoreos terræ motores et solis statores," by Melchior Inchofer, S.J., one of the consultors of the Holy Office, whose opinion on the *Dialogo* is recorded in the MS. Minutes of the Process of 1633. The Professor remarks (p. cxxxvi.) : "L' Inchofer mette altrettanto studio a mostrare che la sentenza fu profferita dal papa ex-cathedra, quanto ora se ne pone nel sostenere l' opposto."

Moreover, the judgment of Rome must outweigh the judgment of individual theologians; and the point I insist on is, that the minimising interpretation of the decree, the interpretation advocated by Dr. Ward and the apologists, is precisely the one that stands emphatically repudiated and denounced by a Pontifical Congregation as involving the gravest error. Before the Inquisitorial sentence of 1633 it might perhaps have been plausibly urged that the decree of the Index was only disciplinary in its scope, that the censures "false and repugnant to Scripture" belonged to the preamble, and not to the decree itself. But to say this in the face of the sentence on Galileo is to say that Rome did not know her own mind, and could not interpret aright her own decisions. The minimising and apologetic view of the decree is, that the Church did not thereby mean to say that it is quite certain, but only highly probable, that heliocentricism is contrary to Scripture; and that she did not intend to deny that the progress of science might change the theological aspect of things. So understood, it is as clear as the sun at noonday that the decision could not, seventeen years afterwards, have shown that it was impossible for the censured opinion to be in any way probable. But this is the very thing Rome, in 1633, declared the decision did show, and pronounced it a most grave error to suppose that it did not—"since *in no manner can an opinion be probable that has already been declared and defined to be contrary to the divine Scripture.*" And it must be noted that the Congregation is expressly referring to the kind of probability Galileo claimed for Copernicanism in the *Dialogo,*—intrinsic probability based on scientific considerations. Did the Congregation mean to say, "Since this opinion has been pronounced contrary to Scripture by a judgment that was not meant to be final, a judgment possibly erroneous, a judgment open to correction by the progress of science, it involves the gravest error to suppose that it can in any manner, even scientifically, be probable"? Yet this is just the nonsense it did mean to talk, if it did not mean its statement in a sense that excludes the apologist's version of the decree. And in the actual sentence the Congregation showed its mind still more plainly, for it implicitly classed the decision with those definitions of the Church, the truth of which it would be heresy to challenge:—"We say, pronounce, and declare that you, the said Galileo, on account of the things proved against you by documentary evidence, and which have been confessed by you as aforesaid, have rendered yourself to this Holy Office vehemently suspected of heresy—that is, that you believed and held a doctrine false and contrary to the sacred and divine Scriptures—to wit, that the sun is in the centre of the universe, and that it does not move from east to west, and that the earth moves and is not in the centre of the universe; *and that an opinion can be held and defended as probable after it has been declared and defined to be contrary to Holy Scripture.*" Such language was, of course, ludicrously inapplicable to the case, unless the decision ought to have been taken as the Church's judgment, and as absolutely true.

Dr. Ward had given certain tests of an ex cathedrâ utterance. Some of them I applied to the Papal decree of the 16th of June, in virtue of which Galileo was compelled to abjure, *de vehementi sub pœna relapsus,* and I still do not see how my critic could consistently escape the conclusion that it was one. "The Pope," he wrote, "never exacts absolute and unreserved assent to any doctrine from individual Catholics, except when he exacts such assent from the whole body of Christians, otherwise he would himself destroy that unity of faith which it is his office to maintain" ("Infallibility and the Council," *Dublin Review,* Jan. 1870, p. 200). If, then, the Pope exacted absolute and unreserved assent from Galileo to the doctrine that heliocentricism is false, he exacted such assent from all Christians, and his Act was, according to Dr. Ward, ex cathedrâ. But that Urban VIII. did exact such assent from Galileo is plain from the minutes of the latter's trial, the sentence pronounced on him, and the terms in which he was made to abjure. Unless Galileo was bound to accept, with the assent of faith, the assertions of Scripture in a geocentric sense, unless he was bound to reject heliocentricism absolutely by an act of faith, as infallibly false, by no possibility could he have lost faith, and, therefore, by no possibility could he have been in "heresy," simply in holding the theory. Upon this point there cannot be the shadow of a doubt. But Urban VIII., by his decree of the 16th of June, ordered a Pontifical Congregation to inform Galileo that heliocentricism had been declared and defined to be contrary to the sacred and divine Scriptures in such sense that his holding it afterwards would be "heresy," in other words would be an offence destructive of his faith as a Catholic. He was called upon to declare on oath that "he had always believed, and did believe, and would for the future believe, all that the Roman Church holds, preaches, and teaches." Now, the Roman Church notoriously holds, preaches, and teaches, and requires all her children to hold, that it is of faith that all opinions opposed to Scripture are false. And therefore Galileo had to confess that he had given Catholics strong reason to think that he had not been true to the faith he had just professed, that he had in fact fallen into "heresy," for he had treated of a certain theory he had been duly and authoritatively informed was contrary to Scripture, in such a way as to lead people to suppose that he really held it. He was made to say: "Because, after this Holy Office had juridically enjoined me to abandon altogether the false opinion which holds that the sun is in the centre of the world and immovable, and that the earth is not the centre and moves; and had forbidden me to hold, defend, or teach in any manner the said false doctrine, and *after it had been notified to me that the said doctrine is repugnant to Holy Scripture*, I wrote, and caused to be printed, a book, wherein I treat of the same doctrine, *already condemned*, and adduce arguments with great efficacy in favour of it without offering any solution of them; therefore I am judged vehemently suspected *of heresy*, that is, *of having held and believed that the sun is the centre of the world and immovable, and that the earth is not the centre and moves*." "Son stato giudicato veementemente sospetto d' eresia, cioè d' aver tenuto, e creduto, che il sole sia centro del mondo, et immobile, e che la terra non sia centro, e si muova." Thus the particular opinions Galileo is suspected of holding, and in holding which he would be in "heresy," because he could not but be aware of their anti-scriptural character, are precisely identified with the opinions that the sun does not move, and that the earth does.* Therefore, to right himself with the Church, and to obtain absolution from the censures he had incurred, he was required in the terms of the established formula for abjuring heresies, "with sincere heart and faith unfeigned, to curse, abjure, and detest the heresies named, and every other heresy and sect contrary to the Holy Catholic and Apostolic Roman Church," *sub pœna relapsus, i.e.* under penalty of being dealt with as a relapsed heretic, should he be convicted of a subsequent fall into the heresies abjured.† Clearly he was called upon, if it was there, to reject altogether from his mind by an act of faith the heliocentric opinion, and eschew it for the future as a "heresy," *i.e.* as an opinion, the falsity of which he could not doubt without doubting the truth of what as a Catholic he was bound to believe was the Word of God. I say, then, that unless Galileo might legitimately appeal in his own mind from

---

* Observe, the authorities did not merely say that Galileo would be in heresy if he held the heliocentric theory; they said, in effect, that his very holding the theory would be in itself heresy, and subject him to the Church's penalties for heresy. When, then, they called upon him to give proof of his faith by abjuring that theory, they must have meant him to abjure it as a heresy, and as absolutely as other heresies are abjured.

† The *abjuratio de vehementi* always carried this penalty with it. A lapse into the heresy abjured, by a legal fiction, counted as a relapse. It was held to cancel the plea on which the culprit had escaped a previous conviction. "Patet ex Constitutione Alexandri IV. Quoad super, *Primum igitur*, ibi: Quod talis si tanquam accusatus, vel suspectus de hæresi, eam in judicio abjuravit, et postea committat in ipsa, censeri debet quodam juris fictione relapsus" (Delbene, *De Officio S. Inquis.*, vol. i. p. 465; see also Sousa, *Aphor. Inquisit.*, lib. ii. c. xli).

It was this circumstance that made the *abjuratio de vehementi* so dreaded: "Sequitur septimo, quod attento jure communi, neque possit Inquisitor sine Episcopo, vel e contra Episcopus sine Inquisitore suspectum vehementer cogere abjurare; quia cum hæc abjuratio sit ignominiosa reo, et ejus consanguineis, illumque reddat obnoxium morti, si in crimen abjuratum incidat, censetur gravissima pœna, quam propterea reus conatur evitare magis quam torturam" (Delbene, *De Officio S. Inquisit.*, vol. ii. p. 22).

the judgment of the Pope and the Congregation as a misrepresentation of the Church's mind—for he could not suppose that the Church would require him to curse, abjure, detest, and absolutely shun for the future as heresies, opinions she did not regard as heresies, and had not made up her mind about—he was placed by Urban VIII. under an obligation of believing with an absolute and unreserved assent, the assent of divine faith, that heliocentricism was false. And if Dr. Ward is right in saying that the Pope never exacts such assent from individual Catholics, except when he exacts it from all Christians, the Pope's Act in the case considered ought to have been regarded as an absolute determination of the question for all Christians.

It remains for me to deal with that most strange contention that the condemnation we have considered was no mistake in the proper sense of the term, because at the time it could not be proved that the earth moves. The plea was suggested long before it was imperatively needed. The judgment, it must be borne in mind, stood almost alone among ecclesiastical decisions in this respect, that it admitted from its subject-matter of being possibly tested by the progress of science; and the question could not but be raised, what if the truth, after all, should turn out to be on the side of Copernicus? Caramuel, the acute casuist, entertained the supposition, and having put into the mouth of an "aliquis" the kind of answer now generally given, dismissed it with contempt in the following words: "Sic forte aliquis responderet, et forte se involveret novis difficultatibus. Ego autem summa cum facilitate me expedio. Assero igitur esse impossibile, quod olim moveri terram demonstrative suadetur. Quid si suaderetur demonstrative? Respondeo: Uno impossibili admisso, non esse absurdum si impossibilia et absurda sequantur" (*Theologia Fundamentalis*, lib. i., n. 28, p. 110). That theologians would ever be driven to occupy their present position, struck Caramuel as an impossibility leading to further impossibilities and absurdities. Others, however, saw more clearly

the advantages of running with the hare and hunting
with the hounds, than the difficulty of the combination.
Among them we find a certain Canon Penitentiary of
St. Peter's, Father Fabri, S.J., whose words have been
referred to by Cardinal Franzelin, Dr. Ward, and others, as
quite oracular. They were originally quoted by Amort
in a passage Dr. Ward has translated as follows:

" Therefore it was that Urban VIII. prohibited under
pain of excommunication the Copernican system, as teme-
rarious and opposed to Scripture in its proper sense,
until some demonstration be adduced by Copernicans
which compels Catholics to recede on a matter of such
grave importance from the proper sense of Scripture, con-
secrated as it is by the judgment of the whole world.
For so is the intention of the Pontifical Bull explained by
F. Fabri, S.J., Canon Penitentiary of St. Peter's at Rome,
where he replies in these words to a certain Copernican:
' It has been asked more than once of your leaders
whether they possessed any demonstration of the earth's
movement?   They have never dared to assert this.
There is no reason, therefore, why the Church should not
understand those texts in their literal sense, and declare
that they should be so understood so long as there is no
demonstration to prove the contrary.   But if any such
demonstration hereafter be devised by your party (which
I do not at all expect), in that case the Church will not at
all hesitate to set forth that those texts are to be understood in a non-natural (*improprio*) and figurative sense,
according to the words of the poet, " terræque urbesque
recedunt."' This reply was inserted in the year 1665 in
the Acts of the English Royal Society" (*Dublin Review*,
July 1871, pp. 162, 163).

The reader may remember that one of Dr. Ward's
arguments proceeded on the assumption that no theologian could contemplate as possible a future discovery
of proof that the earth moves, and hold that the anti-
Copernican decree was put forth under circumstances
that would entitle it to be accounted ex cathedrâ.   Dr.
Ward would not have denied, no Ultramontanist could

deny, that had the anti-Copernican decision been issued
by the Pope in a Bull excommunicating all dissentients,
its claims to be ex cathedrâ would have been irresistible.
Well, here is Amort, a theologian of high standing, under
an impression that the decision was so issued. What
does he do ? Instead of procuring a copy of the supposed Bull, to make himself acquainted with the precise
terms the Pope had used, he accepts without the slightest
hesitation an assurance from a Canon Penitentiary of St.
Peter's to this effect : that the excommunicated Copernican
need not despair ; that the Church—observe, the Church,
not the Congregation of the Index—does not mean
exactly what she says, and that at all events she is open
to conviction. It is true that at present she forbids him
to hold that the earth moves, because the Bible says that
it does not ; but let him demonstrate that it does, and the
Church will at once declare that the Bible says nothing to
the contrary. I gather, then, that had the decree been
ever so clearly ex cathedrâ, theologians might have apolo-
gised for it on the ground they now take. But let us
hear Dr. Ward's exposition and defence of this apology.

"Holy Scripture differs from all other books in the
fact that it is throughout the Word of God ; that every
proposition which it contains is infallibly true, in that
sense in which God intended it." "No inconvenience,
however, arises, nor is there any irreverence towards
God's written Word, though this or that text be understood in a very unobvious sense, if that sense be affixed
in deference to some definite, tangible, objective rule,
the reasonableness of which is sufficiently established"
(*Galileo and the Pontifical Congregations*, p. 155). "God
surely has the right to interpret His own Word, for
you would not deny this right to an ordinary mortal"
(*Authority of Doctrinal Decisions*, p. 143). Now, when
science has demonstrated the overwhelming scientific
probability of Copernicanism, such demonstration may
reasonably be accepted by the Church as God's authoritative explanation of His own language ; even though it
necessitate the understanding that language in a very

unobvious sense. But, on the other hand, if a private individual may ascribe to any text of Scripture any unobvious sense he pleases—not in deference to some definite objective rule proved to be reasonable, but according to his individual bias and caprice,—the same result would practically follow as from an actual denial of inspiration. In Galileo's time heliocentricism was nothing better than an arbitrary scientific hypothesis. If, on the strength of an arbitrary scientific hypothesis, men are at liberty to contradict scriptural texts as understood in that sense which is both the only obvious one and the only one hitherto heard of in the Church, what single text is safe? What is the difference of result, between openly denying the authority of Scripture in general, and explaining away every text one dislikes in particular? Such conduct is a very grave offence against faith. It was impossible, then, in Galileo's time to understand Scripture otherwise than geocentrically, without grave irreverence to the Inspired Word and grave offence against faith. That such was the one genuine interpretation of Holy Writ, was at that time the legitimate and reasonable inference from all cognisable data; and the Congregations did momentous service in authoritatively prescribing that interpretation.

"Putting the matter more compendiously, ... firstly, it is irreverent, unreasonable, unchristian, and uncatholic to interpret Scripture otherwise than according to its one obvious and its one traditional sense, except in deference to some definite, tangible, objective rule, the reasonableness of which is sufficiently established. ... Our second proposition is that Scripture, in its one obvious and in what was then its one traditional sense, declares the geocentric doctrine. Catholics of the present day have become so habituated to Copernicanism that unless they take special pains they can do no kind of justice to the violent shock which that theory inflicted, on the Catholic's most legitimate and laudable prepossessions. Scripture, whether taken by itself, or interpreted by the traditional theology, would not lead its readers so much as to *dream* of any other idea, than that this earth. as it is the moral, so also is it the physical centre of the visible universe. In Scripture statements, the earth is no satellite of the sun, but rather the sun is a satellite of the earth. '*In the beginning* God created the heaven and *the earth*,' whereas not till the fourth day did He create the sun ; and then '·that it might preside over *the earth's* day,' and '*shine over the earth*.' ...

"As one instance of the extreme repuguancy presented by Copernicanism, both to the obvious sense of Scripture and to received theological views, take the ancient doctrine concerning *heaven*. Undoubtedly Copernicanism has not a word to say against the truth, that there is a certain place called 'heaven,' where God is present in some special sense, and which is inhabited by the Son in His Sacred Humanity, by the Blessed Virgin, by all the Beati. But Copernicanism does deny what Scripture, in its one obvious sense, constantly affirms ; viz., that this place is *above the earth*. It is physically impossible—since Copernicanism is true—that heaven can in any imaginable sense be 'above' any given spot on the earth for more than one instant in every twenty-four hours ; while in regard to the earth's surface as a *whole*, it is simply unmeaning in a Copernican's mouth to speak of any place whatever as 'above' it. Yet St. Paul says (Phil. ii. 10), by most inevitable implication, that heaven is *above* the earth. Our Blessed Lord '*raised up* His eyes to heaven,' when He most earnestly prayed to His Father, and declared, '*I ascend* to My Father and your Father,' when He announced His speedy departure to heaven. ...

"... In addition to this uniform drift and implication of Scripture, there are particular texts which we cited in our article of 1865, and which our opponent so criticises (pp. 49-50), as only to make our case the stronger. ... And in real truth it is indefinitely easier to show that Copernicanism is *contradictory* to the Scriptures in their *obvious* sense, than to show that it is *reconcilable* with them in *any* sense. We pointed out, however, in our article of 1865 (pp. 142-3) that there was a precedent of the very highest authority for a Scriptural exposition, even more forced and unobvious than that required for Copernicanism; and this, moreover, within the strict sphere of dogmatic theology; we refer to the Catholic interpretation of Mark xiii. 32. We fully admit, then, that an unobvious exposition of the apparently anti-Copernican texts is possible; and indeed is (as we now know) the true one. We admit that our Blessed Lord, when He looked up to heaven and when He spoke of ascending to the Father, did but accommodate Himself to existing physical beliefs. We admit that the Holy Ghost, for wise purposes—as, for instance, that He might not violently interfere with the healthy slow progress of physical science—permitted the sacred writers to express themselves in language which was literally true as understood by *them*, but was figurative in the highest degree as intended by *Him*. We only say, in accordance with our first proposition, that such an exposition of Scripture would be grossly irreverent, unchristian, and uncatholic, unless there were some overwhelming scientific probability to render it legitimate " (*Galileo and the Pontifical Congregations*, pp. 155-9).

According to these statements the Copernican interpretation of Scripture—the true one, the one intended by God—is intrinsically considered non-reasonable. It is inadmissible on its own merits, and by every sound canon of exegesis. It is so violently opposed to the general drift and implication of Scripture, and to the obvious meaning of particular texts, that nothing short of an express assurance from the Author of Scripture Himself that He really did mean it, would render it legitimate. Such an assurance having been given in these latter days through the conclusions of science, the unobvious and forced character of the exposition is no longer any bar to its reception; on the principle that a man may interpret his own words as he pleases. "God," remarked Dr. Ward, "surely has the right to interpret His own Word, for you would not deny this right to an ordinary mortal " (*Authority of Doctrinal Decisions*, p. 143).

But in Galileo's time God had given no hint that He had meant anything so extremely improbable. Copernicanism at that time was "a random scientific conjecture," with "no leg to stand on." The ecclesiastical authorities were, therefore, only doing their duty in declaring that it was altogether contrary to Scripture.

Desperate indeed must be the cause that stands in need of such monstrous doctrine. Disregarding for the present the grotesque misrepresentation of the scientific status of Copernicanism in Galileo's time, I ask, who admits for a moment that an ordinary mortal may determine *retrospectively* the meaning of his words, and be quit of responsibility for their deceptive effect, on the strength of a subsequent declaration, that he meant the very reverse of what he said or wrote? So far as the Bible professes to teach, and contains assertions that demand belief, assuredly it cannot differ from all other books in this, that its meaning must not be held to depend on the, so to say, objective significance of its language, but on the reserved and unexpressed intention of its author.

How in the name of common sense can what a book really signified in the past be altered, or its then truth be saved, if what it then signified was false, by an interpretation the legitimacy of which depends solely on the production of evidence that did not then exist? If for centuries, according to every known sound and received principle of exegesis, and all the cognisable data that could throw light on the matter, the language of Scripture was so express on the subject as to forbid its being understood otherwise than geocentrically, if nothing short of overwhelming scientific evidence in favour of heliocentricism would justify the opinion that Scripture does not contradict the theory, plainly geocentricism is what the written Word really signifies, and no astronomical discovery can alter the fact.

Is it reasonable to say that while a certain sense is not too much opposed to the letter for the author to mean it, its very opposition to the letter makes it unlawful for those he addresses to suppose him to mean it? Can we, simply by the laws of the language used, be bound to ascribe a meaning to a writer's words he, by those laws under the circumstances, is not bound to give them? Can we call a writer truthful and trustworthy whose words, by themselves, and according to their one legitimate interpretation, oblige us to believe what is false? Is it, then, less than blasphemy to say that God caused Scripture to be so worded as to bind men to error by the force of its terms? That He demanded faith in His Word, and spoke in what theologians call morally undiscoverable equivocations? Who can fail to see that Dr. Ward's estimate of the Copernican interpretation of Scripture is tantamount to a confession, that such an interpretation is a mere makeshift, that the dicta of the sacred writers, properly understood, are really at variance with what we now know to be the truth, and that, therefore, God could not have been their author? And thus it appears that Rome's ill-judged attempt to save the authority of Holy Scripture was an implicit denial of her own dogma on inspiration, and a virtual surrender of the whole position into the enemy's hand.

I say an implicit denial of her own dogma on inspiration, for the Vatican Council has defined it to be a matter of faith that God is the author of the whole of Scripture, and of every part of it—meaning by Scripture all the books enumerated by the Council of Trent as sacred and canonical. Cardinal Franzelin has shown that this doctrine obliges us to hold that God not only caused the human writers of the books named to conceive, with a view to writing them down, those truths, and those truths only, that he meant them to communicate; but further, that God so controlled them in their use of language, that they chose, and chose infallibly, terms fit to express the divinely intended meaning.

"I. In ea formula, (quâ profitemur Deum auctorem librorum sacrorum) ... positive affirmatur, Deum effecisse ut, quas veritates ipse Ecclesiæ per Scripturam tradendas mente comprehendit, easdem *hominis inspirati mens conciperet scribendas, et voluntas ferretur ad eas omnes ac solas scribendas.*

"Dixi eas veritates *omnes et solas* in libro inspirato consignari, quas Deus *auctor libri* mente et voluntate sua comprehendit scribendas. Si enim in libro scriberetur ab homine sententia etiam vera, quam Deus *scribendam* concilio suo non comprehendit et quam proinde homini ad scriptionem non inspiravit, multo magis si in libro Scripturæ, quod theologus recentior de iis quæ nos dicimus *revelata per accidens*, affirmare. ausus est, continerentur aliquæ sententiæ in se non veræ; hujusmodi sententiarum profecto Deus non esset *auctor*, nec proinde illæ essent *verbum Dei*, sed omnino verbum humanum. Atqui *a*) dum S. Concilium Vaticanum post alias geminas Conciliorum et Pontificum definitiones declarat libros veteris et novi Testamenti pro sacris et canonicis ab ipsa Ecclesia haberi 'propterea, *quod Spiritu Sancto inspirante conscripti Deum habent auctorem*,' profecto hæc *conscriptio* intelligitur simpliciter et proinde secundum omnes sententias, quæ ab inspirato scriptore in libro consignatæ sunt; neque enim inspiratio ad conscriptionem interrupta et per intervalla sed ad totam conscriptionem asseritur. *b*) Quando Ecclesia profitetur Deum auctorem *libri sacri et canonici*, hoc *sacrum et canonicum* non minus late patet, quam significatio nominis *Scriptura*. Atqui *Scripturæ* accensentur omnes et solæ sententiæ, quæ ab homine inspirato in libro consignatæ sunt, ac porro in doctrina evangelica et apostolica et in communi Patrum prædicatione expresse singulæ sententiæ, eo quod et ipsæ sunt *Scriptura*, tribuuntur Deo auctori, quod utrumque in Th. I. et II. demonstravimus. Ergo in professione Ecclesiæ et in ejus formula synodali, *Deus est auctor libri sacri et canonici*, intelligitur Deus auctor libri secundum omnes partes quæ sunt Scriptura, ac proinde auctor omnium sententiarum quæ primitus ab homine inspirato sunt libro consignatæ, quoniam hæ omnes et solæ sunt Scriptura. . . .

"II. Operationem divinam, quam explicuimus necessariam, ut vere sit ac dici possit *liber Dei auctoris*, et sine qua Deus *auctor libri* non esset, non eandem requiri quoad *partem materialem* libri ex ipsa notione *auctoris libri* clarum videtur. Est enim ex dictis Deus *auctor libri*, quatenus sua operatione in mentem et voluntatem hominis scribentis efficit, ut hic ea omnia et sola scribat, quæ Deus ipse in libro scribendo *per se* intendit. Hoc autem obtinebitur, ~~omodocumque se habeant ab auctore *per se* non intenta, signa inquam et reliqua quæ diximus *partem materialem* libri, dummodo hæc *apta sint ad sensum ab auctore intentum exprimendum.* Hoc autem ipsum demonstrat, non illam divinam operationem quæ proprie *inspiratio* dicitur, et quæ requiritur pro parte formali libri, necessario etiam extendi ad signa et ad alia *partis materialis;* esse tamen aliquam operationem divinam necessariam etiam pro *parte materiali,* ut Deus infallibiliter sit *auctor libri.* Hæc divina operatio quæ sit, et quæ non sit, nunc inquirimus.

"1. Quoad *signa* seu vocabula evidens est, nec res ipsas h.e. sensa auctoris principis posse esse scripto expressa, *nisi signa eligantur apta ad sensum exprimendum.* Si ergo Deus sua inspiratione rerum et sensuum ita agit in hominem inspiratum ad scribendum, ut liber scriptus *infallibiliter vi ipsius operationis divinæ vere et sincere contineat* sensa Dei, cum ipsa inspiratione cohæreat necesse est seu in ea includatur talis operatio divina, ut homo *scribens non solum actu eligat, sed etiam infallibiliter eligat signa apta* ad res et sententias inspiratas *vere et sincere* exprimendas, atque adeo in signorum aliorumque quæ ad partem materialem pertinent, apta electione reddatur infallibilis. Profecto enim homo mente et voluntate inspiratus quidem ad sensa Dei scribenda, sed in signorum electione plene sibi permissus, maneret fallibilis in exprimendis conceptibus inspiratis; hoc autem ipso non esset infallibiliter consequens, librum sub *tali* inspiratione scriptum esse Scripturam *terminative* inspiratam et verbum Dei. Atqui ut crederetur esse infallibiliter verbum Dei, nunquam aliud argumentum quæsitum est, quam quod scriptor humanus esset inspiratus. Sicut ergo cum inspiratione activa infallibiliter nectitur *inspiratio terminativa* (inspiratum esse) ipsius operis, ita in notione inspirationis activæ includitur operatio divina, qua homo efficiatur infallibilis in exprimendis conceptibus inspiratis, h.e. *in ipsa aptorum signorum ac terminorum electione"* (*De Divina Traditione et Scriptura,* pp. 351, 354-5).

Very good. In Galileo's time, when Copernicanism was condemned, the objected passages of Scripture either were, or were not, adapted to express a meaning not at variance with the theory: if they were, the opinion that they were was reasonable and defensible, apart from any scientific evidence whatever that the earth moved; if they were not, the evidence we have that the earth moves is evidence that God was not the author of those passages. Thus, giving the judgment the very meaning apologists insist is the right one, it implicitly denies the intrinsic reasonableness of the only exposition that can bring certain assertions of Scripture into harmony with science, and in so doing, it implicitly denies that Scripture in all its parts is the written word of God. The doctrine, therefore, of the decision is not only false, but opposed to what the Roman Church holds to be a dogma of the faith.

On Dr. Ward's assertion that " The Copernican interpretation was by no means at that time a rule, the reasonableness of which was sufficiently established, but was, on the contrary, a violent innovation gratuitously trumped up to favour an arbitrary scientific hypothesis," I remark—that the Copernican interpretation of Scripture is justified by the evidence which a consideration of the true scope of Scripture and its cosmographical language as a whole affords, that the sacred writers describe the physical universe from the standpoint of ordinary observation, and refer to it in modes of speech that reflect the imperfect and scientifically inaccurate notions of their day. That they do this, was sufficiently apparent in Galileo's time to be accepted as a reasonable rule of interpretation by every man of science, whether he held the particular theory of the earth's motion, or not. For the obvious earth and heaven of the Bible are neither the earth and heaven as Galileo, nor the earth and heaven as Tycho Brahé and Riccioli, supposed them to be, but, as I have said, the earth and heaven of a much ruder conception of things even than the Ptolemaic. With what consistency could the anti-Copernican appeal to the necessity of keeping to the literal meaning in interpreting passages that relate to the earth's position in the universe, when he could not take even those passages according to the strict letter, and had to abandon the letter altogether in other texts descriptive of the earth's size and shape? The anti-Copernican felt himself quite

at liberty to believe that the death of the King of Baby-
lon did not bring peace literally to the whole earth,
although Isaias says, "How hath the oppressor ceased!
The whole earth is at rest" ("Siluit omnis terra," Is.
xiv. 4-7); and that the fourth kingdom, described in
chap. vii. of the book of Daniel, did not devour literally
the *whole earth*, albeit the prophet says, "It shall devour
the whole earth" ("Devorabit universam terram," v. 29);
and that Alexander did not come literally on the face
of the whole earth, and really go through "even to the
ends of the earth," although it is written (Daniel viii. 5)
that the "he-goat came from the west *on the face of the
whole earth*" ("Veniebat ab occidente super faciem *totius
terræ*"); and that "he (Alexander) went through even to
the ends of the earth" ("Pertransiit usque ad fines terræ,"
1 Mac. i. 3.) Why, then, might not the Copernican hold
that the sun does not really move, although Ecclesiastes
says, "The sun riseth and goeth down"? ("Oritur sol
et occidit," Eccles. i. 5.) Riccioli insists that our Lord
could not possibly have said, "Qui solem suum oriri facit,"
unless the sun really moved; yet he did not suppose that
Sheba was literally at the ends of the earth in relation to
Palestine, because our Lord said (Matt. xii. 42) that "the
Queen of the South came from *the ends of the earth*" ("a
finibus terræ," ἐκ τῶν περάτων τῆς γῆς) to hear the wisdom
of Solomon. Plainly, our Blessed Lord was in both cases
simply using a common mode of speech. In what obvious
and literal sense can it be said that a spherical body has
its four corners? Yet we read in the book of the Apo-
calypse, "I saw four angels standing at the four corners
of the earth" ("Stantes super quatuor angulos terræ," ἐπὶ
τὰς τέσσαρας γωνίας τῆς γῆς (chap. vii. 1).

It was well known in Galileo's time that the moon is
a mere reflector of the sun's light; yet the obvious implication of the letter of Scripture is, that it is in itself a
light. Thus we read, "God made two great lights; the
greater light to rule the day, and the lesser light to rule
the night" (Gen. i. 16). "The sun shall be turned into
darkness, and the moon into blood, before the great and

terrible day of the Lord come" (Joel ii. 31). Deriving its light from the sun, if the sun were turned into darkness, the moon would not be seen at all. Let any one compare the cosmological notions expressed in verses 12-14 of Apoc. vi. with those propounded in any treatise of the seventeenth century that deserves to be called scientific, and he will at once see that something more than the doctrine of the earth's immobility is needed to effect a reconciliation.

Although the case against the ecclesiastical authorities does not, as their apologists would have us believe it does, depend on the value of the scientific argument for Copernicanism when it was condemned, I am unwilling to let Dr. Ward's treatment of that argument pass without a word of protest. In his original remarks on the subject my critic based his unfavourable estimate of the evidence for the earth's movement on a difficulty he supposed Galileo's ignorance made it impossible for him to surmount. Misled by M. Desdouits, a Catholic savant, he thought that the fact that the air has weight was unknown to Galileo, and to every one in Galileo's lifetime, and that therefore no one could then give any sufficient reason for supposing that the earth carries the air with it in its revolution.

"He (Galileo) was unable therefore to complete a theory of his own which he could even reconcile with known facts; and since his opponents had no difficulty whatever in so reconciling theirs, it is not too much to say that his hypothesis, in its then incomplete state, was 'scientifically unlikely,' i.e. that there were stronger grounds for rejecting than for accepting it" (*Doctrinal Decisions*, p. 151).

My answer was Baliani's letter to Galileo, written in 1630, which demonstrates that Galileo was perfectly acquainted with the fact that the air has weight, and was therefore quite able to meet an objection Tycho Brahé himself had discounted.

In his rejoinder, Dr. Ward, without acknowledging his mistake, contends that my own account of the evidence for Copernicanism fully justifies his conclusion. "We understand," he writes, "our opponent to admit that in Galileo's time no cosmical phenomena were known for which geocentricism could not thoroughly account. On the other hand, to our mind the argument from *analogy* is of the vaguest and most shadowy kind, such as is next to worthless when tried by those more rigid and true scientific tests which Mr. Mill has been instrumental in recommending. And as to the argument from simplicity, we can only express surprise that our opponent has condescended to allege it" (*Galileo and the Pontifical Congregations*, p. 160).

Now, I am very far from admitting that in Galileo's time there were no cosmical phenomena known for which geocentricism could not thoroughly account. It is true that if we confine our attention to the phenomena that had to be met in denying the earth's annual motion, a modification of the Tychonic hypothesis might be called an explanation of them. But take this fact, that all the heavenly bodies, the nearest and the most remote—the moon, the planets, the comets, the fixed stars—all appear to revolve round one axis, keeping their relative positions and completing a revolution in the same time, as if they were all in a piece; how could the denier of the earth's diurnal movement account for this phenomenon ? He had nothing to propound but a figment of the imagination, whose *modus operandi* was a mystery. Here heliocentricism had most decidedly the advantage of its rival. It did, and geocentricism did not, undoubtedly fulfil one of the essential conditions of a true theory. The cause to which it assigned the effect to be accounted for would, if it existed, most certainly produce the effect. And the cause assigned was so far exemplified in nature, that the sun was known to revolve on its axis.

Moreover, I do not admit that the argument for considering the earth a planet was nothing more than an argument from analogy. It was not merely that the earth resembled the bodies that revolved round the sun, in certain apparently characteristic particulars, but that it resembled them in a particular there was reason to think was connected, by way of causation, with the fact of their revolution. The earth not only agreed with the planets in being a globular opaque body that derived its light and heat from the sun, but it agreed with them in being a much smaller body than the sun. Now, in every known case of one body revolving round another, it was the smaller body that revolved round the larger. Of course, it was possible that counter-instances would be discovered; but the force of the argument lay in the reasonableness of supposing that the effect was due to the superior attractive power of the body of greater mass. For I would remind the reader that the general notion of gravitation as an attractive force in and between all material bodies, was entertained by scientific men years before Newton saw an apple fall. (See Kepler's *Astronomia Nova*, Introductio, viii.) Kepler's laws, too, were highly suggestive of a force acting from the sun as a centre; and the earth's orbital position and behaviour were apparently just what they should be in accordance with those laws.

To say that these and other considerations on the same side might have turned out to be fallacious, is only to say that heliocentricism was not then entitled to be accounted certainly true. This, of course, I allow; but I think that the evidence even in Galileo's time, considering that no objection could be substantiated, made the theory highly probable, and undeniably something better than " a random scientific conjecture, whose advocates were right by a happy accident." And I can scarcely suppose that Dr. Ward's referee, the "Protestant gentleman of great scientific eminence," would dissent from this opinion.

I concluded my pamphlet with a statement of some inferences, it seemed to me, the case considered would warrant. I have amended them, and have ventured to add the following :

1. Decrees confirmed by, and virtually included in, a Bull addressed to the Universal Church may be, not only scientifically false, but, theologically considered, dangerous, *i.e.* calculated to prejudice the cause of religion, and com-

promise the safety of a portion of the deposit committed to the Church's keeping. Or, in other words, the Pope, in and by a Bull addressed to the universal Church, may confirm and approve with Apostolic authority decisions that are false, unsound, and perilous to the faith.

2. Decrees of the Apostolic See and of Pontifical Congregations may be calculated to oppose the free progress of science.

3. The Pope's infallibility is no guarantee that he may not use his supreme authority to indoctrinate the Church with erroneous opinions, through the medium of Congregations he has erected to assist him in protecting the Church from error.

4. The Pope, through the medium of a Pontifical Congregation, may require, under pain of excommunication, individual Catholics to yield an absolute assent to false, unsound, and dangerous propositions.

We have often been told that the Church could not get on unless she possessed a living judge of controversies, always able to decide questions of importance with infallible truth. Well, but what if the judge need not use his divinely bestowed power when it is wanted? What if, instead of placing himself under heavenly guidance, he may at his discretion listen to earthly counsellors, and decide with scarcely an average amount of human wisdom and prudence?

Holy Scripture is a part of the deposit which, Rome tells us, was committed to her charge, to be faithfully guarded and infallibly expounded. At a time when, through the mistakes of theologians, the progress of science was apparently threatening the authority of Scripture, when Rome, at any rate, thought that authority was threatened, it was surely important, if she spoke at all, that she should speak the truth; if she interposed at all, that she should take the right side, and with a view of the matter that would prevent the possibility of a conflict. Instead of doing so, she confirmed the mistakes of her theologians; she put forward, as God's Word, what was then a doubtful, and what we now know was a false, interpretation of the same; and she proceeded on a principle that events have shown would lead inevitably to the very collision she dreaded.* The Ultramontanist consoles himself with the reflection that these things would not have happened, had the Pope been in his Chair. But, then, why was not the Pope in his Chair?

Dr. Ward (p. 366) says: "When the existing ecclesiastical tribunals are insufficient for putting down some heresy or dangerous error, *then* arises the motive for an ex cathedrâ definition." I submit, ecclesiastical tribunals that might, in .the case supposed, mistake sound doctrine for heresy, and safe truth for dangerous error, most plainly were insufficient for the emergency. "He (the Pope) was naturally persuaded that, by setting in motion the existing Congregations, he had done enough to save the Church from those evils which threatened her." Again I submit, the Pope did something more than set in motion the existing Congregations. With regard, at all events, to the Congregation of 1688, he not only set it in motion, but determined for it the course it was to take; and, to save the Church from the evils that threatened her, it was all-important that the movement to meet them should not be in the wrong direction.

* The principle involves the conclusions that "the heavens and the earth and all that in them is" were made in literally six days (Exod. xx. 11); that the flood was literally universal, and destroyed, outside the ark, literally "every living substance from off the face of the earth" (Gen. vi. 17; vii. 4, 19-23); that the doctrine of evolution in all its forms is a heresy, altogether contrary to the sacred and divine Scriptures. Let any one read Bishop Clifford's letters to the *Tablet* in support of an opinion that the assertions of Holy Scripture are not at variance with the view that the flood was confined to, comparatively speaking, a small area of the earth's surface, and that the great majority of the animals that dwelt on the face of the earth survived it; and let him think of what poor Galileo had to endure for a contention, that, compared with the Bishop's, was most respectful to the letter of Scripture, and he will realise how completely Rome has abandoned the ground on which she once took her stand.

I FIND that I have not noticed two of the three arguments that constitute what Dr. Ward calls "irrefragable evidence;" that I was wrong in saying that the anti-Copernican decrees did not permit the publication of books written to show that there were facts which nothing but the earth's motion would explain. I am not sure that it would not be more respectful to the memory of my distinguished opponent not to draw attention to them; but as others may be of a different opinion, and as my silence may be misunderstood, I will add a word or two on the subject.

On turning to " Galileo and the Pontifical Congregations," at p. 164, the reader will find the following facts given as conclusive proof against me on the particular named. First, "that Bellarmine declared that if a scientific proof of Copernicanism were discovered, Scripture should then be Copernically interpreted; that he said this, moreover, in 1620, at a time when" (according to me) " the Congregations had forbidden that any scientific proof of Copernicanism should be adduced."

I have already met this statement, and have pointed out that there is not a spark of evidence to show that Bellarmine made any such remark, either in 1620, or at any other time after the decree of 1616 was issued. The next fact is that "F. Fabri asks the Copernicans, and says they have frequently been asked, whether they possess any demonstration of their theory; but it is simply impossible he could so have spoken if . . . it was a notorious fact that astronomers were not suffered to publish any such demonstration." What Amort tells us is, that F. Fabri, in a reply to a certain Copernican—probably, as the reply was inserted in the Acts of the English Royal Society, a Protestant—used these words: " It has been asked more than once of your leaders, whether they possessed any demonstration of the earth's movement?" Did Dr. Ward really think that all the leaders of the Coperni-

can party were Roman Catholics, and Roman Catholics so
extremely scrupulous that they would not venture to
answer such a question as that named, if the Pope had
prohibited books written in favour of Copernicanism?
Could not a Roman controversialist at the present day
say to a Darwinian, "It has been asked more than once of
your leaders, whether they possessed a demonstration of
the truth of your theory?" Would his using such words
be conclusive evidence that Rome permitted the advocacy
of the Darwinian hypothesis as true?

"Then," continues Dr. Ward, "consider what was in
fact permitted. Even Copernicus's book was allowed, with
a few verbal changes." Copernicus's book had been within
reach of the ecclesiastical authorities for seventy-three
years, and had hitherto been tolerated. The merits of
the author's hypothesis, as a conception that in a very
simple and accurate way represented the apparent movements of the heavenly bodies, and which was therefore
very useful in astronomical calculations, were fully recognised, even by those that utterly repudiated its pretensions to be the true account of the real order. Under
such circumstances an absolute prohibition of the book
could scarcely have been justified; and so after much
deliberation it was decided that a corrected version of the
De Revolutionibus might be read, the corrections being
sufficient to indicate that it was not permitted in the
sense of an argument for the real truth of the author's
principles touching the earth's position and movement—
those principles were pronounced in the *monitum* "repugnant to Scripture and its true and Catholic interpretation,"
but merely as a treatise that contained "many things very
useful to the state." I fail to see in this case anything
against my contention. It seems to be altogether in my
favour.

But I am reminded "that there is another instance
still more remarkable. Was *Newton* an obscure or feeble
advocate of the Copernican cause?... Yet two religious
were suffered to publish his whole treatment of the
question, with no other reserve than of explaining that

they did not themselves intend to treat heliocentricism
except as an hypothesis." I remark that what they virtually *say* is, that they do *not themselves* intend to treat
heliocentricism as an hypothesis. And when were those
religious suffered to edit the work? In 1742, when it
had been before the scientific world fifty-two years; when
geocentricism as a scientific theory was dead; when ignorance of the *Principia* would have been a disgrace to any
one who professed to be a mathematician and astronomer;
then, indeed, the Minims Le Seur and Jacquier were
permitted to bring out the treatise, with the following
protest attached to the third book:

"Newton in this third book assumes the hypothesis of
the earth's movement. The author's propositions could
not be explained except on the same hypothesis. Hence
we have been obliged to put on a character not our
own. But we profess obedience to the decrees made by
the Supreme Pontiffs against the movement of the earth."

"Newtonus in hoc tertio Libro telluris motæ hypothesim assumit. Auctoris propositiones aliter explicari
non poterant nisi eâdem factâ hypothesi. Hinc alienam
coacti sumus gerere personam. Cæterum latis a Summis
Pontificibus contrà telluris motum decretis nos obsequi
profitemur."

Does this protest show that those decrees by their
own force did not prohibit the publication of the *Principia?* Obviously it shows that, in the opinion of its
Roman editors, they did.

Dr. Ward concludes the paragraph that contains all
this "irrefragable evidence" with the following remark:
"We do not see how it is possible to doubt that scientific
men were allowed to do their very utmost for Copernicanism so long as they explained clearly that they confined themselves to its *scientific* probability, and left to
theology and the Church all concern with its *absolute*
truth or falsehood."

Now we have it on the word of a Pontifical Congregation that what the decree of 1616 was intended to
effect, was the complete suppression of Copernicanism as

E

a pernicious, false, and anti-scriptural theory. And we know on the same authority that it was heresy to believe that the theory was true. And we know from the very terms of the decree that all books that taught the opinion of Foscarinus—*i.e.* that heliocentricism was in harmony with the truth, and was not contrary to Scripture—were absolutely prohibited and condemned. And we know, from the first Index of Alexander VII., that the Church prohibited *all* books that taught the immobility of the sun and the mobility of the earth; and from his second Index, that the prohibition included not only printed books, but treatises in manuscript.* And yet Dr. Ward could see no reason for doubting that a Roman Catholic was quite at liberty to do his very utmost to thwart the Church's purpose; that, so long as he did not say in so many words that the condemned doctrine was true, he might publish any argument he thought a good one that would leave an impression of its truth on men's minds; that, if only he abstained from drawing the conclusion, he might teach it indirectly by putting forward, in the most persuasive way he could, the scientific premises that contained it. Thus he might write a book to show that men of science were well aware that there were certain phenomena that nothing but the earth's movement could explain. He would add, I am not saying, mind, that heliocentricism is true. I am a good Catholic, and know well that it is for the Church to pronounce decisively on the subject; nor do I forget that the ecclesiastical authorities have already declared that the theory is false, and at variance with Scripture; and, of course, I do not venture to contradict them. Nevertheless, I direct your attention to certain facts that, speaking scientifically, we know would not be facts, unless the earth moved.

If Rome, at the time in question, really did allow men to argue in favour of heliocentricism after this fashion, or in any way that would promote the cause of the theory, would there be in history a more glaring exhibition of injustice than her sentence on Galileo?

* See page 95.

The Pontifical Decrees against the Doctrine of the Earth's Movement,

ULTRAMONTANE DEFENCE OF THEM.

Rome in the 17th century stigmatising as false and anti-scriptural opinions she has since learnt from the English-man Newton to recognise as true and sound, certainly seems to be a fact opposed to a theory that can be expressed as follows: "Rome, let it never be forgotten, is commissioned to teach England and Germany, not England or Germany to teach Rome. So far as any Englishmen or Germans are at variance with what is authoritatively inculcated in Rome, they are infallibly in error."[*] But we have been told that the contradiction is only in appearance; "that the decision referred to, was not a mistake on a matter of doctrine, nor of principle; that it was not uttered by the Pope ex cathedrâ, but by Cardinals, for whom no one claims infallibility; that it was a mere disciplinary enactment, very necessary for its times; that it afforded true doctrinal guidance to con-temporary Catholics, and was, in fact, the one legitimate application of Catholic principle to the circumstances with which it dealt."[†] In the following pages I will endeavour to vindicate the relevancy of the objection, and show that all such answers as those just mentioned, ignore the true history of the case.

The judgment, the effect of which is in question, was

[*] *Authority of Doctrinal Decisions*, by W. G. Ward, p. 96.
[†] Ibid. p. 186.

first communicated to the Church in the following well-known decree, which I transcribe from the *Elenchus Librorum prohibitorum*, published at Rome in 1640, under the editorship of Capiferreus, who, be it observed, was secretary to the Index when the edict was issued:

" *Decretum Sacræ Congregationis Illustrissimorum S. R. E. Card. a S. D. N. Paulo Papa V. Sanctaque Sede Apostolica ad Indicem Librorum, eorumdemque permissionem, prohibitionem, expurgationem, et impressionem, in universa Republica Christiana specialiter deputatorum, ubique publicandum.*

"Cum ab aliquo tempore citra, prodierint in lucem inter alios nonnulli libri, varias hæreses atque errores continentes, ideo Sacra Congregatio Illustriss. S. R. E. Cardd. ad Indicem Deputatorum, ne ex eorum lectione graviora 'in dies damna in tota Republica Christiana oriantur, eos omnino damnandos atque prohibendos esse voluit; sicuti præsenti Decreto penitus damnat et prohibet, ubicumque et quovis idiomate impressos aut imprimendos. Mandans, ut nullus deinceps, cujuscunque gradus, et conditionis sub pœnis in Sacro Concilio Tridentino, et in Indice Librorum prohibitorum contentis, eos audeat imprimere aut imprimi curare, vel quomodocunque apud se detinere, aut legere. Et sub iisdem pœnis quicunque nunc illos habent, vel habuerint in futurum, locorum Ordinariis, seu Inquisitoribus, statim a præsentis Decreti notitia exhibere teneantur. Libri autem sunt infrascripti, videlicet:

" Theologiæ Calvinistarum Libri tres, auctore Conrado Schlusserburgio.

" Scotanus Redivivus, sive Comentarius Erotematicus in tres priores libros Codicis, &c.

" Gravissimæ quæstionis de Christianarum Ecclesiarum, in occidentis præsertim partibus, ab Apostolicis temporibus ad nostram usque ætatem continua successione et statu, historica explicatio. Auctore Jacobo Usserio, S. Theologiæ in Dubliniensi Academia apud Hybernos Professore.

" Frederici Achillis Ducis Wirtemberg. Consultatio

de Principatu inter Provincias Europæ, habita Tubingiæ in Illustri Collegio, anno Christi 1613.

"Donnelli Enucleati, sive Comentariorum Hugonis Donelli, de Jure Civili in compendium ita redactorum, &c.

"Et quia etiam ad notitiam præfatæ Sacræ Congregationis pervenit, falsam illam doctrinam Pythagoricam, divinæque Scripturæ omnino adversantem de mobilitate Terræ, et immobilitate Solis, quam Nicolaus Copernicus de revolutionibus orbium celestium, et Didacus Astunica in Job etiam docent, jam divulgari et a multis recipi; sicuti videre est ex quadem epistola impressa cujusdam Patris Carmelitæ, cui titulus, Lettera del R. Padre Maestro Paolo Antonio Foscarini Carmelitano sopra l' opinione de' Pittagorici, e del Copernico, della mobilità della Terra, e stabilità del Sole, et il nuovo Pittagorico Sistema del Mondo, in Napoli per Lazzaro Scoriggio 1615; in qua dictus Pater ostendere conatur, præfatam doctrinam de immobilitate Solis in centro Mundi, et mobilitate Terræ, consonam esse veritati, et non adversari Sacræ Scripturæ: Ideo ne ulterius hujusmodi opinio in perniciem Catholicæ veritatis serpat, censuit dictos Nicolaum Copernicum de revolutionibus orbium, et Didacum Astunica in Job suspendendos esse donec corrigantur. Librum vero Patris Pauli Antonii Foscarini Carmelitæ omnino prohibendum, atque damnandum; aliosque omnes Libros pariter idem docentes, prohibendos, prout præsenti Decreto omnes respective prohibet, damnat, atque suspendit. In quorum fidem præsens Decretum manu et sigillo Illustrissimi et Reverendissimi D. Cardinalis Sanctæ Cæciliæ Episcopi Albanensis signatum et munitum fuit, die 5. Martii 1616.

"P. Episc. Albanen. Card. Sanctæ Cæciliæ.

Locus Sigilli.

"F. Franciscus Magdalenus Capiferreus, Ord. Prædicat. Secretarius."

I subjoin a translation of the part we have to do with:

"Since it has come to the knowledge of the above-named Holy Congregation that that false Pythagorean doctrine, altogether opposed to the divine Scripture, on the mobility of the earth and the immobility of the sun,—which Nicolas Copernicus in his work *De Revolutionibus Orbium Cœlestium*, and Didacus a Stunica in his commentary on Job, teach,—is being promulgated and accepted by many, as may be seen from a printed letter of a certain Carmelite father, entitled *Lettera del R. Padre Maestro Paolo Antonio Foscarini sopra l' opinione de' Pittagorici, e del Copernico della mobilità della Terra e stabilità del Sole, &c.*, wherein the said father has endeavoured to show that the aforesaid doctrine of the immobility of the sun in the centre of the universe, and the mobility of the earth, is consonant to truth, and is not opposed to Holy Scripture; therefore, lest an opinion of this kind insinuate itself further to the destruction of Catholic truth, this Congregation has decreed that the said books—*Nicolas Copernicus De Revolutionibus* and *Didacus a Stunica on Job*—be suspended till they are corrected; but that the book of Father Paul Antony Foscarini the Carmelite be altogether prohibited and condemned, and all other books that teach the same thing; as the present decree respectively prohibits, condemns, and suspends all. In witness whereof this decree was signed and sealed with the hand and seal of the most illustrious and Reverend Lord Cardinal of Saint Cæcilia, Bishop of Albano, on the 5th day of March 1616."

Now the Ultramontanist does, and, as we shall see, must, admit, that if this decree had been accompanied with the clause "quibus Sanctissimo per me infrascriptum relatis, Sanctitas sua decretum probavit et promulgari præcepit," its declaration ought not, on his theory, to have been the mistake it was; but appearing as it did without that notice, it had not, he contends, the slightest pretensions, from the principles of his school, to be accounted anything more, than a confessedly fallible utterance. Looking back, then, and calculating what, humanly speaking, the chances were, he would fain persuade us that the erroneous decision under the circumstances, so far from being a difficulty to him, is a positive argument in his favour. "How truly remarkable," exclaims Dr. Ward,

"that no adverse decision was put forth for which any
one could even claim infallibility! that the decree issued
was Congregational, and not Pontifical! . . . Who can
fail to see in all this the finger of God?"*

"Merito," says M. Bouix, "alligari valet dicta condemnatio ad confirmandam pontificiæ infallibilitatis prærogativam. Nam si hoc totum Galilæi negotium perpen-
datur, cuidam supernæ providentiæ tribuendum est, quod
decreto Cardinalium non accesserit solita clausula de
pontificia confirmatione aut speciali mandato. . . . . Cur
præcise quoad tale decretum omissum est, quod omitti non
solet? Cur illa omissio quam sic testatur commissarius
Sancti Officii, Pater Olivieri, *on avait omis de faire approuver
le décret par le Pape?* Id fortuito casui forsan quis adscri-
bendum existimabit! At mihi liceat altiorem causam
autumare. Cum nempe decretum istud errorem con-
tineret, singulari sua providentia præpedivit Christus ne a
Romano Pontifice ex cathedra confirmaretur; et sic illæsa
remaneret cælitus concessa inerrantiæ prærogativa" (Bouix,
Tractatus de Papa, vol. ii. p. 476).

The simple truth of the matter is this:—The custom
referred to is, comparatively speaking, quite modern; and
the notion that a decree of the Index in 1616 ought by
usage to have had the clause, involves an anachronism,
most discreditable to the author of a treatise on the
Roman Curia. To prove this sufficiently for my purpose,
I need only refer to the work from which I have taken the
decree. The *Elenchus* of Capiferreus was, as I have said,
published in 1640. It professes to give "omnia decreta
hactenus edita." It contains, in fact, twenty-five Congregational edicts. Not one has the clausula. So much
for the insinuation that the omission in the case before us
was something quite providentially exceptional; something that might have indicated an abnormal deficiency
of authority. I now raise these two questions:—First, is
it true that the Ultramontanist's general doctrine on the
authority of Congregational decrees justifies his relegating
the decision in question to the class of confessedly fallible

* *Authority of Doctrinal Decisions,* pp. 182, 183.

utterances? Secondly, does not the denial of this judgment's infallibility involve an abandonment of the only
ground upon which the infallibility of a decree with the
clause can be reasonably defended?

On turning to M. Bouix's *Tractatus de Curia Romana*[*]
—a work Dr. Ward most warmly recommends to our
notice—we learn that there are three kinds of Congregational decrees: 1. Those which the Pope puts forth in his
own name after consulting a Congregation. 2. Those
which a Congregation puts forth in its own name with
the Pope's confirmation, or express order to publish.
3. Those which a Congregation with the Pope's sanction
puts forth in its own name, but without the Pope's confirmation or express order to publish. Decrees of the
first and second class, we are told, are certainly ex
cathedrâ, and to be received with unqualified assent under
pain of mortal sin.

According to Zaccaria—a very great authority—even
decrees of the last class are not fallible, in the sense that
they can ever condemn as erroneous a doctrine which is
not so. To this M. Bouix demurs; and his reasons for so
doing place his own position in the clearest possible light.
As Dr. Ward has misrepresented that position, and as
M. Bouix himself tries to shuffle out of it when he comes
to deal with the difficulty under discussion, I will quote
what he says, at full length, and in his own words.

"Privilegium inerrantiæ Romano Pontifici divinitus
concessum ipsi omnino personale est; neque potest
Summus Pontifex prærogativam illam aliis communicare.
Textus enim Sacræ Scripturæ, et traditionis documenta
quæ Summi Pontificis infallibilitatem adstruunt, simul
aperte hanc prærogativam exhibent tanquam ipsi exclusive
ex divina institutione propriam. Jam vero si infallibilia
forent decreta dogmatica ex mandato *generali* a Sacris
Congregationibus edita, incommunicabilis non esset infallibilitatis prærogativa, nec soli Romano Pontifici exclusive
propria. Nam per ejusmodi *generale* mandatum depu-

° Pars iii. cap. vii. p. 471.

tantur quidem Cardinales ad judicandum de doctrina; et
auctoritate Pontificia hoc suum munus explent; at judicia
Cardinalium *non sunt proprie judicia ipsiusmet Pontificis,
quamdiu Pontifex ea in particulari non cognoverit et assensum
dederit.* Nemo enim potest judicare de veritate aut
falsitate alicujus propositionis, nisi propositionem illam
cognoscat, et proprii intellectus actu eam veram aut falsam
pronuntiet. Ergo si intervenerit dumtaxat generale
mandatum, et *non supervenerit ipsummet Pontificis proprie
dictum judicium,* dicta decreta dogmatica non erunt simul
judicia Cardinalium et Pontificis, sed dumtaxat judicia
Cardinalium. Ergo si forent infallibilia, infallibilitas hæc
inhæreret Sacræ Congregationi, et Pontifex S. Congregationem generaliter ad judicandum de doctrina deputando,
ei suam communicaret inerrantiæ prærogativam.

" *Objicies* 1º.—Per generale mandatum quo Romanus
Pontifex Sacræ Congregationi Inquisitionis committit ut
de doctrina pronuntiet, simul ei confert auctoritatem suam
Pontificiam; ergo et auctoritatem infallibilem.

" *Respondeo.*—Ei confert auctoritatem Pontificiam quoad
eam partem quæ est communicabilis et delegabilis, concedo : quoad eam partem quæ nequit communicari et
delegari, nego. In iis scilicet quæ ad regimen ecclesias-
ticum pertinent et a voluntate pendent, potest Summus
Pontifex auctoritatem suam delegare. Et de facto pluribus
Sacris Congregationibus legislativam suam potestatem in
certis materiis contulit Sedes Apostolica; ita ut univer-
saliter obligent decreta disciplinaria a Sacris Congregationibus, intra fines concessæ ipsis facultatis edita, perinde
ac si ab ipso Pontifice immediate prodiissent. Et tunc
applicandum venit axioma, *quod facit per alios perinde est
ac si per se faceret.* At vero potestas infallibiliter pro-
nuntiandi de dogmate, ipsimet Pontifici, id est, judiciis ab
ipsiusmet intellectu elicitis divinitus alligata est. Ut
nempe infallibile sit judicium de alicujus propositionis
veritate aut falsitate, necesse est ut ipsemet Pontifex ad
hanc propositionem attendens, de ea pronuntiet. Ergo
nequit Pontifex hanc inerrantiæ prærogativam aliis communicare seu delegare. Ergo quantumvis Sacram In-

quisitionis Congregationem ad pronuntiandum de doctrina deputaverit, infallibile non erit ullum hujus congregationis decretum *nisi Pontifex hocce decretum suo proprio et proprie dicto judicio firmaverit.* Ejusmodi autem proprie dictum Pontificis judicium in generali mandato non includitur.

"*Objicies* 2°.—Per generale mandatum, id est, deputando Sacram Congregationem ad pronuntiandum de doctrina, Summus Pontifex *sua facit* ejusdem Congregationis decreta dogmatica. Ergo perinde valent decreta illa ac si forent ipsiusmet Pontificis judicia. Ergo infallibilia censenda sunt.

"*Respondeo.*—Per solum generale mandatum Summus Pontifex nequaquam *sua facit* dicta Sacræ Congregationis judicia, eo modo qui ad infallibilitatem requirereter. Nam, ex dictis, ad infallibilitatem requireretur, ut quod de unaquaque propositione Sacra Congregatio pronuntiavit, idipsum Romanus Pontifex de iisdem propositionibus proprie dicto suo judicio pronuntiaret. Porro ejusmodi proprie dictum Pontificis judicium non adest per solum generale mandatum, ut patet : adest vero per *speciale* ipsius mandatum aut confirmationem, ut infra ostenditur.

"*Objicies* 3°.—Rem evinci rationibus Zaccariæ supra relatis.

"*Respondeo.*—Etsi de iis sim qui clarissimum virum summa æstimatione prosequantur, fateor tamen dictas rationes haud mihi peremptorias videri. Arguit nempe *primo* ab experientia, qua teste, nullum adhuc intervenit dictæ speciei decretum, erroneum aliquid definiens. Esto ita sit (a quo expendendo hic abstinemus, ne quis nobis Galilæi condemnationem et alia nonnulla obstrepat). At potuit ita contingere ob notam illam Eminentissimorum Patrum sapientiam, qua solent arduas de dogmate quæstiones Summo Pontifici remittere, ut eas suo supremo ac infallibili judicio dirimat; ita ut suo nomine et absque Pontificis confirmatione aut speciali mandato non definierint, nisi quæ alias jam omnino plana erant. Arguit *secundo* ex eo quod, ad majorem conciliandam Pontificis ex cathedra loquentis definitionibus reverentiam divina dispositione cautum censendum sit, ut etiam dicta Congregationum decreta inerrantiæ privilegio donarentur. At quamvis negare non audeam ita revera fuisse divinitus dispositum, dico ˉtamen id rigorose non probari. Non enim necesse fuit ut Pontifici ex cathedra loquenti reverentiam conciliaret Deus, omnibus qui excogitari possunt modis; at satis fuit provideri sufficienti aliquo modo; qualis profecto fuit, Pontificis ex cathedra loquentis inerrantiam revelasse, et Ecclesiæ suæ omnino certam fecisse " (Pars iii. cap. vii. pp. 475-7).

The argument comes to this : Scripture and tradition show that the gift of inerrancy attaches by divine promise to the Pope as a strictly personal prerogative. He cannot therefore delegate it to others. Hence a decision to be infallible must represent the Pope's own judgment on the point at issue. The general order under which the Congregations act invests them, indeed, with authority to decide, but, containing no judgment on the point to be decided, cannot render the decree they publish in virtue of that order, Papal in the sense required to guarantee it from error. And as to Zaccaria's appeal to the testimony of experience—that a Congregation has never yet put forth an erroneous decision—the fact, if it be a fact, may be accounted for by supposing that the Cardinals have always been wise enough to consult the Pope, before issuing a decree in a difficult case.

Beyond the shadow of a doubt, the only decisions covered *by this reasoning* are those that are not Papal judgments at all—those that cannot in any true sense be said to represent the Pope's own mind on the question at issue. But it is admitted that the condemnation of Copernicanism was, *and was known to be,* a Papal judgment, and that the decree of 1616 was the result of Paul V.'s having applied his own mind to the very point to be settled. "Paul V.," says Dr. Ward, "undoubtedly united with the Congregation of the Index in solemnly declaring that Copernicanism is contrary to Scripture."* Undoubtedly, then, that declaration is positively disqualified for being placed under

* *Authority of Doctrinal Decisions,* p. 144.

the only class of utterances M. Bouix has any right to call *confessedly* fallible. Now let us see whether its infallibility can be denied without abandoning the only ground on which the ex cathedrâ character of decrees of the second class can be defended, granting, for argument's sake, that they are decrees that are published with the clause.

Why does the Papal confirmation, or express order to publish, argue infallibility? Because, says M. Bouix, either fact proves that the judgment published is the Pope's own decision for the Church:—

"Infallibilia sunt dicta decreta in posteriori etiam casu, id est, quando *eduntur* quidem *nomine Sacræ Congregationis*, sed de *speciali mandato* Papæ, aut accedente ipsius confirmatione.

"1°. In casu accedentis Pontificiæ confirmationis, patet decretum ipsimet Pontifici esse attribuendum; *si quidem illud confirmando suum facit.* Et cum aliunde sit dogmaticum et publicetur, per illud Summus Pontifex universalem Ecclesiam docere censendus est; ac proinde, infallibile sit ejusmodi decretum necesse est.

"2°. Infallibile etiam est decretum dogmaticum, *Sacræ Congregationis nomine editum,* si publicetur de *speciali mandato* Pontificis. Hoc ipso enim quod Summus Pontifex, habita notitia de aliquo ejusmodi decreto dogmatico, vult et jubet illud publicari, *ipsum approbat ac suum facit. Proinde ipsemet judicat ac definit id ipsum quod in decreto definitur.* Ergo non minus valebit istud decretum quam si a Pontifice ipso immediate et ipsius nomine ederetur et publicaretur. Ergo et per ipsum censendus est Pontifex tanquam universalis Doctor, ac proinde infallibiliter, de dogmate pronuntiare" (Pars iii. c. vii. p. 480).

A moment's reflection will show that M. Bouix stands pledged to the following principle:— Whenever the Pope passes judgment on a question of doctrine, and causes that judgment to be communicated to the Church, whether directly, in his own name, or *indirectly, in the name of a Congregation* he judges ex cathedrâ, and infallibly. Dr.

Ward does not admit this, and gives a very different account of the matter.

" The Pope," he says, "exercises two different functions, not to speak of more: (1) that of the Church's Infallible Teacher; and (2) that of her Supreme Governor. The former he can in no sense delegate; but of the latter he may delegate a greater or less portion, as to him may seem good. Moreover, in either of these characters he may put forth a doctrinal decree; but with a somewhat different bearing. If he put it forth as Universal Teacher, he says, in effect, ' I teach the whole Church such a doctrine;' and the doctrine is of course known thereby to be infallibly true. But if he put forth a doctrinal decree as Supreme Governor, he says, in effect, ' I shall govern the Church on the principle that this doctrine is true.' That the doctrine so recommended has an extremely strong claim on a Catholic's interior assent, is the very thesis which we are presently to urge; but, of course, it is not infallibly true; because no Papal dicta have that characteristic, unless the Pope utters them in his capacity as Universal Teacher " (*Auth. of Doc. Dec.* pp. 130, 131).

Thus, according to Dr. Ward, the question turns *on the mode of publication*. Papal dicta *put forth* by the Pope in his capacity of Universal Teacher are ex cathedrâ, and to be accounted infallibly true. Papal dicta *put forth* by the Pope in his capacity of Supreme Ruler are not ex cathedrâ, but confessedly fallible. How, then, does it follow from the Pope's having ordered a Congregation— which, mark, Dr. Ward tells us, p. 132, represents him exclusively in his capacity of Supreme Governor—to publish even a *doctrinal* decree *in its name*, that he has spoken ex cathedrâ? And most clearly it follows from the distinction laid down, that a Papal judgment communicated to the Church *solely through the medium of a disciplinary decree is confessedly not* ex cathedrâ. Let us hear what the Pope himself has to say upon this subject. On the 8th of January 1857 the works of a distinguished theologian and philosopher, Günther, were condemned by what, according to all theological rule, was nothing more than a disciplinary decree.* Günther himself submitted, and so did many of his followers. Some of them, however, contended that a mere disciplinary decree was not conclusive against the soundness of their master's tenets. Whereupon, to set them right, his Holiness, on the 15th of June, the same year, addressed a Brief to the Archbishop of Cologne:

"Nos quidem, pro Apostolici Nostri ministerii officio, nullis unquam parcentes curis nullisque laboribus, ut fidei depositum Nobis divinitus concreditum integrum inviolatumque custodiatur, ubi primum a pluribus Venerabilibus Fratribus spectatissimis Germaniæ Sacrorum Antistitibus accepimus, non pauca Güntheri libris contineri, quæ ipsi in sinceræ fidei et catholicæ veritatis perniciem cedere arbitrabantur; nulla interposita mora, eidem Congregationi commisimus, ut ex more, opera ejusdem Güntheri accurate diligenterque excuteret, perpenderet, examinaret, ac deinde omnia ad Nos referret. Cum igitur ipsa Congregatio Nostris mandatis obsequuta suoque munere functa, omnem in hoc, gravissimo sane maximique momenti negotio, curam et operam scite riteque collocaverit, nullumque prætermiserit studium in Güntheriana doctrina accuratissimo examine noscenda ac ponderanda, animadvertit plura in Güntheri libris reperiri omnino improbanda ac damnanda, utpote quæ catholicæ Ecclesiæ doctrinæ maxime adversarentur. Hinc, rebus omnibus a Nobis etiam perpensis, eadem Congregatio Decretum illud suprema Nostra Auctoritate probatum, Tibique notissimum edidit, quo Güntheriana opera prohibentur et interdicuntur. Quod quidem Decretum, Nostra Auctoritate sancitum Nostroque jussu vulgatum, sufficere plane debebat, ut quæstio omnis penitus dirempta censeretur, et omnes qui catholico gloriantur nomine clare aperteque intelligerent sibi esse omnino obtemperandum, et sinceram haberi non posse doctrinam Güntherianis libris contentam, ac nemini deinceps fas esse doctrinam iis libris traditam tueri ac propugnare, et illos libros sine debita facultate

* Conf. Bouix, *Tractatus de Curia Romana*, pars iii. cap. vii. p. 471.

legere ao retinere. A quo quidem obedientiæ debitique obsequii officio nemo immunis propterea videri censerique poterat, quod in eodem Decreto vel nullæ nominatim propositiones notarentur, vel nulla certa stataque adhiberetur censura. Ipsum enim per se valebat Decretum, ne qui sibi integrum putarent, ab iis quæ Nos comprobavimus, utcumque discedere."

The Pope says in effect, "The original judgment on Günther's works, because it was Papal, clearly ought to have been accounted absolutely decisive, *although it was presented to the Church solely through the medium of a disciplinary decree;* in other words, *although it was put forth by the Pope exclusively in his capacity of Supreme Ruler.*" This certainly looks like a thoroughgoing indorsement of the principle we have extracted from M. Bouix, in opposition to Dr. Ward's. The former gentleman, indeed, in his *Tractatus de Papa*, to save himself from the consequences of his own doctrine when applied to the decree of 1616, catches at "the clause," and quietly argues as if it were the same thing as a Bull or Brief of confirmation. But the assumption is false. The clause is a notice *not from the Pope himself*, but from the Secretary of the Congregation, who certifies, not that his Holiness approved the decree *publicly*, but in his the attestor's presence; and ordered it to be published:—in whose name? *In the name of the Congregation.* And mark, in the case of Günther's condemnation, the decree itself contained no assertion whatever that the works condemned *were unsound.* "Yet," says Pius IX., "that decree, sanctioned by our authority and promulgated by our command, plainly ought to have sufficed *that the whole question* be judged entirely settled, and all who boast of the Catholic name should clearly and distinctly understand that complete obedience was to be paid to it; and that the doctrine contained in Günther's books could not be accounted sound (sinceram haberi non posse). . . . Nor could any one deem himself excused from rendering such due tribute of obedience and submission on the ground

that in the decree no propositions were marked by name,
no determinate censure was expressed. For the decree
itself was quite sufficient to prevent any one's thinking
himself at liberty to depart in the slightest degree from
what we approved."

I submit, then, that the more obvious meaning of the
Pope's teaching is, that the question does not turn on any
such distinction as Dr. Ward imagines, but that Catholics
ought to regard it as infallibly certain that an opinion is
unsound, if the Church has received an official intimation
that the Pope has declared it to be so. I have only, then,
to show that the Church received an official intimation
that the decision against Copernicanism was Papal, and
that judgment's claims on Ultramontane ground to be
accounted infallibly true will be evident.

In the first place, I contend that the decree of 1616 by
itself was such a notice; for it emanated from a Congregation acting under the provisions of a Bull which distinctly gave the Church to understand, that decisions of
the kind would invariably be examined and ratified by the
Holy See before publication, and would go forth clothed
with Papal authority. With regard to all the Congregations Sixtus V. had said,

"Congregationes quindecim constituimus, singulisque
certa negotia assignavimus, *ita ut graviores difficilioresque
consultationes ad nos referant.* . . . Et quoniam divinis
oraculis admonemur, ubi multa consilia, ibi salutem, adesse
eædem Congregationes pro earum arbitrio viros Sacræ
Theologiæ, Pontificii Cæsareique juris peritos, et rerum
gerendarum usu pollentes in consultationibus advocent
atque adhibeant; ut causis, quæstionibus, et negotiis
quam optime discussis, quæ Dei gloriæ animarumque
saluti, et justitiæ atque æquitati consentanea maxime
erunt, decernantur: *graviora vero quæcunque ad nos vel
successores nostros deferantur, ut quid secundum Deum expediat, ejus gratia adjuvante, mature statuamus.*"

And with special reference to the Congregation of the
Index:

"Quare ut Cardinales, qui ad libros prohibendos expur-

Jesus Christ, and that of His most glorious Mother Mary ever Virgin, by this our definitive sentence we say, pronounce, judge, and declare, that you, the said Galileo, on account of the things proved against you by documentary evidence, and which have been confessed by you as aforesaid, have rendered yourself to this Holy Office vehemently suspected of *heresy*—that is, of having believed and held a doctrine which is false and contrary to the sacred and divine Scriptures—to wit, that the sun is in the centre of the world, and that it does not move from east to west, and that the earth moves, and is not the centre of the universe; and *that an opinion can be held and defended as probable after it has been declared and defined to be contrary to Holy Scripture.* And consequently that you have incurred all the censures and penalties decreed and promulgated by the sacred canons and other constitutions, general and particular, against delinquents of this class. From which it is our pleasure that you should be absolved, provided that, with a pure heart and faith unfeigned, you in our presence first abjure, curse, and detest, the above-named errors and *heresies,* and every other error and heresy contrary to the Catholic and Apostolic Roman Church, according to the formula which we shall show you.

"And that this your grave and pernicious error, and transgression remain not altogether unpunished, and that you may be the more cautious for the future, and *be an example to others to abstain from offences of this sort,* we decree that the book of the Dialogues of Galileo Galilei be prohibited by public edict; and you we condemn to the prison of this Holy Office during our will and pleasure; and, as a salutary penance, we command you for three years, to recite once a week, the seven Penitential Psalms; reserving to ourselves the power of moderating, commuting, or taking away altogether, or in part, the above-mentioned penalties and penances."

And Galileo had to abjure in the following terms:

"I, Galileo Galilei, son of the late Vincenzio Galilei of Florence, aged seventy years, appearing personally before this court, and kneeling before you, the most eminent and reverend Lord Cardinals, Inquisitors-General of the universal Christian Republic against heretical pravity, having before my eyes the most holy Gospels, and touching them with my hands, swear that I always have believed, and now believe, and with God's help will always believe, all that the Holy Catholic and Apostolic Roman Church holds, preaches, and teaches. But because, after this Holy Office had juridically enjoined me to abandon altogether the false opinion which holds that the sun is in the centre of the world, and immovable, and that the earth is not the centre, and moves; and had forbidden me to hold, defend, or teach in any manner, the said false doctrine; and *after it had been notified to me that the said doctrine is repugnant to Holy Scripture,* I wrote and caused to be printed a book, wherein I treat of the same doctrine *already condemned,* and adduced arguments with great efficacy in favour of it, without offering any solution of them; therefore I am judged vehemently suspected of *heresy,* that is, of having held and believed that the sun is the centre of the world and immovable, and that the earth is not the centre, and moves. Wherefore, desiring to remove from the minds of your Eminences, and *all Catholic Christians,* this vehement suspicion legitimately conceived against me, *with a sincere heart and faith unfeigned, I abjure, curse, and detest, the above-named errors, and heresies, and generally every other error and sect contrary to the above-mentioned Holy Church;* and I swear that for the future, I will neither say, nor assert by word of mouth, or in writing, anything to bring upon me similar suspicion. And if I shall know any heretic, or one suspected of heresy, I will denounce him to this Holy Office, or to the Inquisitor, or Ordinary of the place in which I may be. Moreover I swear, and promise, to fulfil, and observe entirely, all the penances that have been or shall be imposed on me by this Holy Office. And if— which God forbid—I act against any of these said promises, protestations, and oaths, I subject myself to all the penalties and punishments which the sacred canons, and other constitutions, general and particular, have enacted, and promulgated against such delinquents. So help me God, and His holy Gospels, which I touch with my hands.

"I, Galileo Galilei above-named, have abjured, sworn, promised, and bound myself as above; in token whereof I have signed with my own hand this formula of my abjuration, and have recited it word by word."

Thus did Rome's supreme Pontifical Congregation, established, to use the words of Sixtus V., "tanquam firmissimum Catholicæ fidei propugnaculum . . . cui ob summam rei gravitatem Romanus Pontifex præsidere solet," known to be acting under the Pope's orders, announce to the Catholic world that it had been ruled that the Papal declaration of 1616 was to be received, not as a fallible utterance, but as an absolute settlement of the question, as an expression of the mind of the Holy Catholic and Apostolic Church of Rome, and that the Holy See regarded the opinion condemned thereby as nothing less than heresy. Can it, then, be denied that the decision against Galileo, in virtue of Sixtus V.'s Bull on the one hand, and Rome's strong words and acts in 1633 on the other, had as good a title to be accounted infallibly true as the decision against Günther plainly had, in virtue of the clause-bearing decree of 1857? I turn to M. Bouix for an answer:

"Objicies," he says: "In sententia contra Galilæum pronuntiata, supponitur ab ipsomet Papa condemnatam fuisse doctrinam de motu terræ. Ibi enim de quadem testificatione quam Galilæus a Cardinali Bellarmino impetraverat sic habetur. 'In qua testificatione dicitur, te non abjurasse neque punitum fuisse, sed tantummodo denuntiatam tibi fuisse *declarationem factam* a Domino Nostro, et promulgatam a Sacra Congregatione Indicis, in qua continetur, doctrinam de motu terræ et stabilitate solis contrariam esse Sacris Scripturis.' Igitur condemnatio Copernicani systematis, quæ exprimitur in decreto 5 Martii 1616, *facta fuit* ab ipsomet Summo Pontifice.

"Respondeo: Facta est ab ipso Pontifice, ast edenda et publicanda solo nomine cardinalium, et quin accesserit Pontificis confirmatio aut speciale mandatum, concedo. Facta est a Pontifice, id est, edita fuit et publicata nomine Pontificis, vel ei accessit attestatio de publica Pontificis confirmatione aut speciali mandato, nego. Decreta scilicet, quæ solo nomine cardinalium eduntur, non fiunt plerumque, præsertim si magni momenti sint, nisi postquam ipse Summus Pontifex quæstionem expendit, et decreta hæc jam approbavit ac edi mandavit. Unde in eo sensu dici possunt ab ipso facta. Sed ejusmodi approbatio et mandatum Pontificis, de quibus nulla fit attestatio publica, remanent actus *privati ; sunt nempe Pontificis privatam personam agentis, non autem decernentis ut Pontificis et ex cathedra.* Quæstio est num Galilæi et Copernicani systematis condemnationem suam fecerit aliquis Romanus Pontifex per litteras apostolicas, vel per solitam clausulam et publicam attestationem de ipsius confirmatione aut speciali mandato. Id a nullo Papa peractum dicimus; nec contrarium probant objecta verba" (*Tractatus de Papa*, vol. ii. pars 11, pp. 474-5).

In accepting this solution, we commit ourselves to the following absurdities:

1. That the Pope uniting with a Congregation to make a law for the universal Church does not, *ipso facto*, act in his official capacity as the Church's supreme Legislator.

2. That the Supreme Pontiff referring in a Bull to the Pope in such terms as these, "Ubi *nobis* retulerint *nostra auctoritate* rejiciant"—"graviora quæcunque *ad nos vel successores nostros* deferantur, *ut quid secundum Deum expediat, ejus gratia adjuvante, mature statuamus,*" may be supposed to mean the Pope *in his private capacity.*

3. That a Pontifical Congregation acting under the Pope's orders in testifying that an opinion *since its condemnation* by the Pope is to be regarded as a *heresy,** to

* "Hæresis," says De Lugo, "est secta seu divisio, et hæreticus est sectarius, quia secat et dividit unitatem Ecclesiæ, seque a reliquo Ecclesiæ corpore

be renounced among the *other* errors and heresies opposed
to the Holy Catholic and Apostolic Roman Church, does
not in effect attest that the Holy See has condemned
that opinion.

Is the Pope's public confirmation the only one to be
reckoned official? And must a decree be published *in
the Pope's own name* to have claims to infallibility? Then,
I submit, the Günther decree's title to be accounted ex
cathedra is bad. A document cannot attest more than it
says, or obviously implies, and the clause attached to the
Günther decree neither said, nor implied that the Pope
had *publicly* confirmed that decision, nor that he had
ordered it to be published *in his name*. Nor did it assure
the Church that the Pope had given that decree any
more authority than Sixtus V. assured the Church the
Pope would give every Congregational decree on a matter
of grave importance; certainly no more authority than
the sentence of 1633 implied the Pope had given the
decision of 1616. The question, When does the Pope act
as Pope, must be determined, not by what theologians
in a difficulty choose to assert, but by the language and
practice of the Pope himself. And I contend that the
language of Sixtus V.'s Bull, and the practical inter-

---

et sensu dividit, sectando et amplectendo proprium sensum et opinionem
contra id quod Ecclesia sentit.

"Ecclesia proponit totam Scripturam Sacram ut indubitanter a fidelibus
credatur, tanquam vera Dei revelatio; *addit insuper pœnas speciales non
contra omnes non credentes, sed contra hæreticos, hoc est, contra eos, qui
contra communem Ecclesiæ sensum aliter credunt ac a Deo revelatum sit.*
Quamvis ergo aliqui vel aliquis subtilius et melius scripturam legens pene-
tret et percipiat sufficienter sensum in aliqua scripturæ clausula contentum,
quem communiter alii non ita poterant percipere, atque adeo aliter sentiens
peccet contra Dei fidem; *non tamen incurrit pœnas specialiter ab Ecclesia
statutas, quæ non sunt contra omnes non credentes, sed contra aliter credentes, contra communem Ecclesiæ sensum.*

"In foro externo non punietur ille pœnis corporalibus hæreticorum quoties ipse ostendet Doctores Catholicos communiter non tradere eum sensum
tanquam certum, sed aliquos eum negare, alios fateri non esse omnino
certum, nec pertinere ad fidem Catholicam. Imo licet aliqui dicant id esse
de fide, si tamen ipse pro se afferat alios graves Doctores id negantes, non
damnabitur tanquam hæreticus, ut observavit Hurtado, addens hæresim
propriam talis esse naturæ ut ab omnibus viris doctis et Catholicis censeatur hæresis post diligentem criminis cognitionem" (*De Virt. Div. Fidei,*
disp. xx. sect. ii. 60, 62, 63).

pretation it received for many years, eminently in the case
under discussion, prove that the Pope has claimed to
decide questions for the Church *as Pope, through a Congregation,* without either Bull, Brief, Apostolic Letter, or
clause.*

With regard to the conduct of the Inquisition in 1633,
M. Bouix holds that the tribunal had no right to require
Galileo to abjure his opinions, inasmuch as they had not
been condemned ex cathedrâ; but he thinks the Congregation proceeded in ignorance, not malice :†

"Porro in hoc mihi videter dictum tribunal aliquid
humani passum esse ; suæ scilicet potestatis limites
excessisse, et injustum exstitisse, non quidem ex *pravo
ullo affectu, sed ex errore.* Enimvero dictam Galilæi
opinionem nondum infallibilis Ecclesiæ auctoritas, id est,
Summus Pontifex ex cathedra loquens, erroneam aut
hæreticam pronuntiaverat. Ipsa autem Inquisitionis congregatio poterat quidem de ista opinione judicare, eique
notas theologicas quæ justæ viderentur (etiam hæreseos)
inurere, et prohibere sub pœnis ne quis eam *externe* pro-
pugnaret. At hoc ipsius judicium, utpote cui nondum
accesserat Summi Pontificis ex cathedra loquentis confirmatio, remanebat fallibile. Proinde, nec Galilæus, nec
quivis alius, poterat juste adigi ut *interne* et ex animo
illi judicio adhæreret.‡ Unde Sacra Inquisitionis Congregatio, Galilæum adigendo ut *corde sincero et fide non*

* Speaking of the Declarations of the Congregation of the Council of
Trent, Fagnanus says : "Quotiescunque emergentia dubia nondum decisa
resolvuntur, ad præscriptum Constitutionis Sixti V. de omnibus consuevit
fieri relatio Papæ a Cardinali Præfecto vel a Secretario Congregationis, ut
ego ipse diu observavi, *licet id in declarationibus exprimi nec opus sit, nec
semper soleat*" (*De Const. c. Quoniam,* tom. i. p. 134).

† Monsignor Marini, on the contrary, is in ecstasies over the sentence,
and thinks that perhaps no judicial act ever came up to it in wisdom and
justice : "Non possiamo, a rendere il debito elogio alla giustizia, sapienza, e
moderazione della stessa Inquisizione, non affermare non esservi forse mai
stato nè così giusto nè così sapiente atto giudiziario che questa sentenza"
(*Galileo e l' Inquisizione,* p. 141).

‡ Dr. Ward, on the contrary, dogmatically asserts that no Catholic is
permitted to hold the opinion here advanced. I cannot think that he has
succeeded in vindicating his own doctrine on the subject. It is certainly
quite irrelevant to the present issue; for plainly the assent demanded
from Galileo by Urban VIII. was of the most absolute kind—the assent of
faith.

ficta opinionem de terræ motu abjuraret, idque antequam cardinalium hac in re judicium confirmasset ex cathedra loquens Summus Pontifex, potestatis suæ limites excessit, ac injuste egit " (p. 485).

As if a Congregation composed of Cardinals, carefully selected by the Pope to try a difficult case, might be credited with a piece of theological ignorance that would disgrace a candidate for ordination! M. Bouix is forgetting the Munich Brief.

"Incidit in Scyllam cupiens vitare Charybdim."

But how about the Pope's share in the business? The Congregation did not exceed its rights in the opinion of the Pope, and whatever injustice it committed lies at Urban VIII.'s door. M. Bouix is prepared for something of the kind being said.

" Objicies :—Hac in re nihil egit Inquisitionis tribunal nisi assentiente et dirigente Urbano VIII.; ergo, si admittatur error, in ipsum Papam refundendus est.

"Respondeo : Distinguo antecedens : nisi assentiente Urbano VIII. *quatenus doctore privato*, transeat; quatenus loquente ex cathedra, nego. Item, distinguo consequens : refundendus error in ipsum Papam, *quatenus doctorem privatum*, transeat; quatenus loquentem ex cathedra, nego. Unde ad *summum ex objectione sequeretur ipsum etiam Urbanum VIII. quatenus doctorem privatum, hac in re deviasse* " (p. 486).

So the Head of a Congregation is not to be held officially responsible for the acts it does with his full knowledge and consent! But M. Bouix writes as if he knew nothing of those extracts from the original minutes of the process M. de l'Epinois published some three years ago in the *Revue des Questions Historiques.** In the face of that evidence he might as well deny that Galileo's trial took place at all, as say that the Pope did not preside over it from first to last in his official capacity. It was

* M. de l'Epinois has since republished them with greater accuracy, in a work entitled *Les Pièces du Procès de Galilée.* They have also been edited by Professor Berti and others.

not that the Congregation did nothing "nisi assentiente et dirigente Urbano VIII.," but "nisi jubente et mandante Sanctissimo."

The facts were as follows:—

The *Dialogo* was published at the beginning of the year 1632. Late in the spring it reached the authorities at Rome. Towards the end of the summer his Holiness ordered a commission to examine the work, and draw up a report of the circumstances under which the imprimatur had been obtained. The following list was returned of the points forming the corpus delicti: observe No. IV.:—

"Conforme *all' ordine della Santita vestra* si è distesa tutta la serie del fatto occorso circa l' impressione del libro del Galilei quale poi è stato impresso in Fiorenza. .... Nel libro poi ci sono da considerare come per corpo di delitto le cose sequenti:

"I. Aver posto l' imprimatur di Roma senz' ordine e senza participar la publicatione con chi si dice aver sottoscritto.

"II. Aver posto la prefazione con carattere distinto, e resala inutile come alienata dal corpo dell' opera, et aver posto la medicina del fine in bocca di un sciocco, et in parte che ne anche si trova, se non con difficoltà, approvata poi dall' altro interlocutore freddamente, e con accennar solamente e non distinguer il bene che mostra dire di mala voglia.

"III. Mancarsi nell' opera molte volte e recedere dall' hipotesi, o asserendo assolutamente la mobilità della terra e stabilità del sole, o qualificando gli argumenti su che la fonda per demostrativi e necessarii, o trattando la parte negativa per impossibile.

"IV. *Tratta la cosa come non decisa, e come che si aspetti e non si presupponga la definizione.*

"V. Lo strapazzo degl' autori contrarii, e di chi più si serve S. Chiesa.

"VI. Asserirci e dichiararsi male qualche uguaglianza nel comprendere le cose geometriche tra l' intelletto umano e divino.

"VII. Dar per argomento di verità che passino i Tolemaici ai Copernicani, e non e contra.

"VIII. Haver mal ridotto l' esistente flusso e reflusso del mare nella stabilità del sole e mobilità della terra non esistenti.

"Tutte le quali cose si potrebbono emendare se si giudicasse esser qualche utilità nel libro del quale gli si dovesse far questa grazia" (MS. minutes of the process, *Les Pièces du Procès*, par Henri de l'Epinois, pp. 44, 47).

The immediate result of this representation was an injunction to stop the sale of the *Dialogo*, and sequestrate all obtainable copies (Marini, p. 117). And on the 23rd of September a letter was sent by the Pope's command to the Inquisitor-General of Florence, bidding him serve Galileo with a summons to present himself before the Commissary of the Holy Office in Rome some day during the ensuing month.

"Sanctissimus mandavit Inquisitori Florentiæ scribi, ut eidem Galileo nomine S. Congregationis significet quod per totum mensem Octobris proximum compareat in Urbe coram Commissario Generali S. Officii, et ab eo recipiat promissionem de parendo huic præcepto, quod eidem faciat coram notario et testibus, ipso tamen Galileo hoc penitus inscio, qui in casu quo illud admittere noluit, et parere non promittat, possint id testificare, si opus fuerit." (Vat. MS. fol. 394, v°.).

On the 1st of October, Galileo acknowledged the execution of this order, and promised obedience (MS. p. 398). At the same time, he did not mean to go if he could help it. On the 13th he wrote to Cardinal Barberini expressing his surprise " that his enemies had been able to persuade the authorities that his work deserved suppression; and the pain he felt at being summoned to Rome as though he had committed some grave fault. In all his writings he had ever kept the interests of the Church steadily in view; and though he would rather die than disobey, he trusted that his great age, the state of his health, and what he must suffer in a journey to Rome, might be considered sufficient reasons for the Congregation to grant him at least a reprieve."[*]

Niccolini, not without misgivings, and mainly in deference to Father Castelli's advice, presented the letter. In writing back to Galileo on the subject, he points out the necessity of absolute submission; that he must not think of defending his opinions, but must be prepared to make any retractation the Holy Office chose to demand:

"Quanto poi al negozio, creda pure che gli sarà necessario non entrare in difesa di quelle cose che la Congregazione non approva, ma deferire a quella, e ritrattarsi nel modo che vorranno i Cardinali di essa, altrimenti troverà difficoltà grandissime nell' espedizione della causa sua, come è intervenuto a molti altri; *ne parlando cristianamente, si può pretendere altro che quello che vogliono loro, come tribunal supremo che non può errare.*"[†]

In the mean time the ambassador left no stone unturned to get the order rescinded; but in vain. Ginetti, one of the Cardinals, and Monsig. Boccabella, the Assessor of the Holy Office, listened to his representations, and said nothing. He then tried to soften the Pope.

"I went this morning," he writes in a despatch dated the 13th of November, "into all the circumstances of the case with his Holiness, and tried to stir up his compassion for the poor old man. I asked him if he had seen his letter to Cardinal Barberini. The Pope said that he had, but could not dispense with his coming to Rome. Niccolini hinted that he might die on the road. 'He may come slowly,' said the Pope; 'pian piano in a litter, and have anything he pleases to lessen the discomforts of the journey; but he must be examined here in person; and God forgive him for having got into such a scrape after I, when Cardinal, had extricated him on a former occasion!'"[‡]

On the 20th of November, the Inquisitor at Florence

* *Opere di G. G.* Fl. ed. vol. vii. p. 7.
† Ibid. vol. ix. p. 305.   ‡ Ibid. vol. ix. p. 429.

wrote to say "that he had again cited Galileo before him, that the latter had expressed his willingness to obey, but pleaded his age, his bodily ailments, that he was then under medical treatment, and so forth. He had exacted from him a promise, in the presence of witnesses, to start at the end of a month," "non so poi se l' eseguira." "If he does not," his Holiness replied, "he must be made to do so."

"9 Dec. 1632. Sanctissimus mandavit Inquisitori rescribi, ut post elapsum terminum unius mensis assignatum Galileo veniendi ad Urbem, omnino illum cogat, quibuscunque non obstantibus, ad Urbem accedere" (MS. fol. 402).

On the 18th of December the Inquisitor notified that his Vicar on visiting Galileo had found him confined to his bed, declaring himself quite incapable of undertaking the journey to Rome in his then state of health. A certificate was forwarded, signed by three of the most eminent medical men in Florence, to the effect that Galileo was suffering from hernia, and could not be moved without peril to his life. But his Holiness and the Congregation were incredulous, and returned the following stringent order:

"30 Dec. 1632, a Nativitate. Sanctissimus mandavit Inquisitori rescribi quod Sanctitas sua et Sacra Congregatio nullatenus potest et debet tolerare hujusmodi subterfugia; et ad effectum verificandi an revera in statu tali reperiatur, quod non possit ad urbem absque vitæ periculo accedere, Sanctissimus et Sacra Congregatio transmittent illuc commissarium una cum medicis, qui illum visitent, ac certam et sinceram relationem faciant de statu in quo reperitur; et si erit in statu tali ut venire possit, illum carceratum et ligatum cum ferris transmittat. Si vero causa sanitatis et ob periculum vitæ transmissio erit differenda, statim postquam convaluerit, et cessante periculo, carceratus, et ligatus, ac cum ferris, transmittatur. Commissarius autem et medici transmittantur ejus sump-

tibus et expensis, quia se in tali statu et temporibus con-
stituit, et tempore opportuno ut ei fuerat præceptum venire
et parere contempsit" (MS. fol. 409).

Galileo's friends begged him to start at once. On the
20th of January he managed to get well enough to begin
the journey in one of the Grand Duke's litters. On the
13th of February he reached Rome; and the next day
paid his visit to the Commissary of the Holy Office.

It has been contended that the Pope was under an
impression that Galileo meant to hold him up to ridicule
in the *Dialogo*, and that mortified vanity prompted his
conduct. To my mind, the evidence does not warrant
the charge. What Urban did fully agrees with what he
said—that he was taking up the case on purely public
grounds, from a conviction that the interests of religion
and the faith were at stake; and that, sorry as he was to
pain an old friend, and one standing so high in the favour
of the Grand Duke, he could not do less than prohibit
the doctrine of the *Dialogo*, and make an example of the
author.[*]

Every one admits that Galileo during his trial was
treated with unusual indulgence; and his sentence was a

[*] Conf. the following extracts from Niccolini's despatches (*Opere di G. G.
Fl. ed. vol. ix.):

"Roma, 5 Sett. 1632 : Rispose che questo era il manco male che se gli
potesse fare, e che si guardasse di non esser chiamato al S. Offizio, e d' aver
decretata una Congregazione di Teologi e d' altre persone versate in diverse
scienze, gravi e di santa mente, che a parola per parola vanno pesando ogni
minuzia, *perchè si trattava della più perversa materia che si potesse mai
aver alle mani,* tornando a dolersi d' essere stata aggirata da lui e dal
Ciampoli. *Poi mi dissi, che io scrivessi per ultimo al Padrone Serenissimo,
che la dottrina era perversa in estremo grado* " (vol. ix. pp. 421-2).

"Roma, 18 Sett.: Replicai di supplicarla umilmente di nuovo a considerare, che il Signor Galilei era matematico di S. A., suo stipendiato, e suo
servitore attuale, e per tale ricevuto anche universalmente; e S. S. replicò,
*che per questo anche era uscita dall' ordinario con noi, e che ancora il
Signor Galilei era suo amico, ma che queste opinioni furono dannate circa a
16 anni sono;* e che anch' egli è entrato in un gran ginepreto, nel quale
poteva far di meno, perche son materie fastidiose e pericolose; e *che questa
sua opera in fatti è perniciosa, e la materia è grave più di quel che S. A.
si persuade ;* . . . . anzi soggiunse che si cercasse di star in poco avvertiti, e
questo io lo significassi onninamente a S. A., che il Signor Galilei, sotto pre-
testo di certa scuola di giovanetti che tiene, non vada imprimendo loro

much lighter one than he had reason to expect. Let us look at things from the standpoint of the court.* It assumed, we must bear in mind, that the doctrinal question had been settled, and that the decision of 1616 was absolute. The issues before it were these two,—Had Galileo wilfully transgressed the order he was under, not to treat of Copernicanism in any manner? Did he hold, and had he written advisedly in favour of that con-

---

qualche opinione fastidiosa e pericolosa, perchè aveva inteso non so che; e che di grazia S. A. vi stesse attenta e vi facesse star vigilante qualcheduno, affinchè non le seminasse qualche errore per gli stati, da doverne ricever de' fastidi" (p. 427).

"Roma, 13 Nov.: Io dissi che l' approvazione quì del libro aveva cagionato tutto questo, perchè mediante la sottoscrizione e l' ordine dato all' Inquisitor di Firenze s' era camminato al sicuro e senza sospetto in questo interesse; ma fui interrotto col dirmi, che il Ciampoli ed il Maestro del S. Palazzo s' eran portati male, e che quei servitori che non fanno a modo de' padroni son pessimi familiari; perchè in dimandare al Ciampoli spesse volte quel ch' era del Galilei, non le aveva mai risposto altro, se non bene, senza passar più avanti in dirle che il libro si stampava, quando pur S. S. ne aveva subodorato qualche cosa, *tornando a dire di trattarsi di pessima dottrina*" (p. 430).

"Roma, 18 Marzo: Cominciai questa mattina il mio ragionamento con Sua Santità dall' uffizio di rendimento di grazie . . . . mi disse . . . . e che Iddio gli perdoni a entrar in queste materie, tornando a dire che *si tratta di dottrine nuove, e della Scrittura Sacra*, e che la meglio di tutte è quella di andar con la comune; . . . . *che il Signor Galilei è stato suo amico, ed hanno insieme trattato e mangiato più volte domesticamente, e dispiacerle d' averlo a disgustare, ma trattarsi d' interesse della fede e della religione*" (pp. 436-7).

"Roma, 9 Aprile: E questa mattina avendone anche parlato a S. Beatitudine, dopo i dovuti rendimenti di grazie della partecipazione anticipata, di che ha voluto favorirmi, s' è doluta la Santità Sua che sia entrato in questa materia, *la quale da lei è stimata gravissima e di consequenza grande per la religione*" (p. 439).

"Roma, 18 Giugno: Ho di nuovo supplicato per la spedizione della causa del Signor Galilei, e Sua Santità mi ha significato ch' ell' è di già spedita, e che di quest' altra settimana sarà chiamato una mattina al S. Uffizio per sentire la resoluzione o la sentenza . . . . Mi replicò . . . . perche aveva fatta volentieri ogni abilità al Signor Galilei in riguardo all' amore, che porta al Padron Serenissimo: *ma che quanto alla causa non si potrà far di meno di non proibire quell' opinione, perchè è erronea e contraria alle Sacre Scritture dettate ex ore Dei*" (pp. 443-4).

After Galileo's death, when rumours of an intention to erect a monument to the philosopher in the Church of Santa Croce had reached the Pope's ears, his Holiness objected: "Che non era punto di esempio al mondo, che S. A. facesse questa cosa, mentre egli è stato qui nel S. Uffizio *per un' opinione tanto falsa e tanto erronea;* con la quale anche ha impressionati molti altri costà, e dato anche scandalo tanto universale al Cristianesimo *con una dottrina stata dannata*" (Venturi, vol. ii. p. 324).

* See the minutes of the trial in *Les Pièces du Procès de Galilée*, par Henri de l'Epinois, pp. 61-94.

demned opinion ? If so, according to the former ruling
of the court, his crime was heresy.

Galileo's answer on the first count was, that he had
completely forgotten that the order contained the words
"teach in any manner." And to render this statement
credible, he produced Bellarmine's record of the order
without the words.* He had taken, he said, that certificate as a complete account of the transaction it referred
to. Nor had it occurred to him to tax his memory on
the subject. Further, since it was obvious that the
judgment notified to him was one and the same thing
with the declaration of the Index, he had not supposed
himself to be under any special restriction, and therefore
had not thought it necessary to mention the order when
he applied for the *imprimatur*.

With regard to the second point he absolutely denied
that he had meant the *Dialogo* to be a defence of Copernicanism. He granted that vain-glory, and the desire
men have to show off their cleverness in arguing even for
propositions they allow to be false, had led him to give
an appearance of strength to the Copernican side; but
his real intent had been to show the *inconclusiveness* of
the argument for the theory. And he begged the court
to allow him to add a dialogue to the work, to make the
thing quite unmistakable.

But the evidence was dead against him. And we
cannot wonder that the consultors of the Holy Office—
Augustinus Oregius, Melchior Inchofer, and Zacharias
Pasqualigus—protested against his defence, and declared
their conviction that the accused had held, defended, and
taught, the theory of the earth's motion.

It remained for the Pope to determine what should be
done. He must have been morally sure that Galileo had
not spoken the truth ; and had it been his object to crush
the man, he might, I take it, have condemned him for
heresy on the data he had. Instead of doing this, he
decreed as follows :

* The Cardinal may have purposely omitted the words for Galileo's sake,
that his enemies might not twit him with being under special restraint.

Galileo was to be questioned about his intention. He was to be threatened with the torture.* If he stood the threat, he was to be condemned, after making the abjuration " de vehementi " in a full assembly of the Holy Office, to imprisonment during the pleasure of the Sacred Congregation. An injunction was to be laid on him never again to treat of the heliocentric theory, for and against, by word of mouth or in writing, under pain of being dealt

---

* The torture seems to have been threatened to extort a confession, when, from age or other circumstances, its actual infliction was not intended.

" Si inquisitores habent vehementem opinionem contra reum, *quamvis extra processum, possunt eum verbaliter terrere, minando torturam, etiamsi legitima indicia non procedant;* quia hoc non est torquere, nisi sit persona timida.

" Rursus, torquere non possunt minores 14 annis " (ita *Delrius*, lib. v. sect. ix. contr. Villadiego, pol. i. 3, n. 322). " *Possunt tamen tales terrere ducendo sub equuleo absque ligatura* " (ita *Miránda*, ibid. initio).

" Et tandem non possunt torquere senes. Sed senectus non est annorum numero computanda (ut docet Villagut, Prax. Crim. tit. v. c. xxi. n. xii. requirens annos 60), sed valetudine, robore, qualitate delicti et delinquentis, inquisitorum arbitrio. Quando vero torquere non possunt, posse terreri, ait Cavalcanus, p. iii. n. 126 " (*Diana, Summa*, pars post. n. 108, 140, 141).

It is not true that the Popes only permitted the use of torture; they enjoined it, as M. Bonix perfectly well knows, under threat of excommunication, and promoted it by express decrees. See Constitutions, " Ad extirpanda," of Inn. IV., Alex. IV., Clement IV., and the following : " Inhærendo decretis alias per felicis recordationis Paulum Papam Quartum, D. N. Pius V. decrevit omnes et quoscunque reos confessos et convictos de hæresi, pro ulteriori veritate habenda, et super complicibus, fore torquendos arbitrio D. D. Judicum " (quoted by Carena, *de Sancto Off*. pars ii. p. 65). The Holy Office, it was held, could less than any court dispense with this method of getting at the truth, and for the following reasons : " Inquisitores," says Diana, " debent esse proniores ad torturam, *quia crimen hæresis est occultum et difficilis probationis.* Simancas addit aliam rationem, quia confessio rei in casu hæresis non solum reipublicæ sed ipsimet heretico proficit " (*Summa*, pars post. 104). " Quod hæretici torqueantur pro ulteriori veritate &c. clarissimum est, et ab omnibus pro indubitato præsupponitur. Quoniam hæresis *delictum est in mente residens, et occultum,* singulare habet hoc Officium S. Inquisitionis ut per tormenta judices violatæ Religionis possint se certificare, an bene, an male, de fide senserit reus in hoc Sancto Tribunali inquisitus."

" Quod confitentes se hæreticalia verba protulisse, sed *intentionem hæreticam* sese habuisse negantes, *quod super ista intentionis qualitate torqueantur,* et torquere soleant in hoc Sancto Officio, nemo in hoc Sacro Tribunali, vel mediocriter versatus, ignorat . . . Ratio hujus conclusionis est quia *de intentione istius rei non potest Ecclesia (quæ de occultis non solet judicare) sese certificare nisi per tormenta, et ob id reos super intentione ista torquere solet* " (Carena, *de S. Officio*, pars ii. pp. 62, 63). Nevertheless I believe that, as a rule, the physical torments of the Inquisition were less severe than those of most secular courts of the day. Certainly we find the best authorities discountenancing and inveighing against novel and excessive kinds (cf. *Pegna in Eymeric. Direct.* pars iii. p. 594).

with as a relapsed heretic. The *Dialogo* was to be prohibited. And that all might know these things, his Holiness commanded the Congregation to send copies of the sentence to all the Nuncios Apostolic, to all the Inquisitors of heretical pravity,* and expressly to the Inquisitor of Florence, who was to summon a number of mathematical professors to hear it read publicly.

Ms. fol. 451. "Die 16 Junii 1633. Galilei de Galileis, de quo supra, proposita causa, Sanctissimus decrevit ipsum interrogandum esse super intentione, etiam comminata ei tortura, et si sustinuerit, previa abjuratione de vehementi in plena congregatione S. Officii, condemnandum ad carcerem arbitrio Sacræ Congregationis, injuncto ei ne de cætero scripto, vel verbo, tractet amplius quovis modo de mobilitate terræ, nec de stabilitate solis, et e contra, sub pœna relapsus. Librum vero ab eo conscriptum, cui titulus est: Dialogo di Galileo Galilei Linceo, prohibendum fore. Præterea, ut hæc omnibus innotescant, exemplaria sententiæ desuper ferendæ transmitti jussit ad omnes Nuncios Apostolicos, et ad omnes hereticæ pravitatis Inquisitores, ac præcipue ad Inquisitorem Florentiæ, qui eam sententiam in ejus plena congregatione, accersitis etiam et coram plerisque mathematicæ artis professoribus, publice legat."†

Accordingly, on the 21st of June, Galileo underwent a final examination with respect to his intention in writing the *Dialogo*.‡

* In this part of the order the Pope not obscurely intimated his will that the Copernically-minded Catholics should be forced to yield assent to the decision of 1616. For the local tribunals of the Inquisition were to take their tone from the Supreme Court.

"Jura ubique clamant majores Ecclesiæ causas, et præsertim quæ articulos fidei tangunt, ad Sedem Apostolicam esse referendas. Ergo privati civitatum Inquisitores, si tutius et securius tractare omnia cupiunt, cum leges deficiunt, aut etiam obscuræ sunt leges, stylum et consuetudinem Supremi Senatus Inquisitionis Romanæ, quæ ceterarum caput est, consulant et sequantur. In hac enim nullum est erroris periculum; nam præterquam quod a sapientissimis judicibus et vigilantissimis causæ fidei tractantur, quotidie etiam Summum Pontificem consulere licet, cujus judicium quantam in rebus fidei habeat auctoritatem exploratissimum est apud Catholicos" (*Franciscus Pegna in Eymeric. Direct. Inquisit. De Auctorit. Extrav. p. 149*).

† *Les Pièces du Procès de Galilée*, par Henri de l'Epinois, p. 98. For the version of this decree in Gherardi's documents see Appendix E, p. 124.

‡ *Les Pièces du Procès*, pp. 93, 94.

He was asked to say whether he held, or had held, and since when, that the sun is in the centre of the universe, and that the earth is not the centre, but moves, and with a diurnal movement.

He replied that before the determination of the Congregation of the Index, and until he received an order to the contrary, he had suspended his judgment on the matter, and had thought it an open question whether the truth lay with Ptolemy or Copernicus, there being no reason in the nature of things why either might not be right. But when his superiors decided the point he ceased to doubt, and held, and continued to hold, the opinion of Ptolemy, that the earth is fixed, and that the sun moves.

The Congregation submitted that his having written the *Dialogo* was inconsistent with this statement, and urged him to speak the truth.

He said that his object in writing the *Dialogo* was to exhibit the astronomical and physical arguments that might be advanced on both sides of the controversy; and to show that, as reason could not settle the question, recourse must be had to a higher teaching—"alla determinatione di più sublimi dottrine." He concluded by again asserting that he did not hold the condemned opinion, and had not held it since its condemnation.*

He was then warned that the presumption was so strong against him, that if he did not confess, the court must have recourse to the remedies the law provided for such cases.

He repeated his assertion that he had not held the opinion of Copernicus since he had been ordered to give it up: "I am in your hands, and you must do what you think fit."

He was then told, in plain terms, that if he did not speak the truth, he would be put to the torture.

* Dr. Ward seems to think that Galileo was probably speaking the truth. I think he will change his mind after referring to the philosopher's letter to Prince Cesi, 23 Sept. 1624; to Cesare Marsili, 7 Dec. 1624; to Elia Diodati, 15 Jan. 1633; conf. also Niccolini's letter, 9 April 1633.

"I am here," he said, "to obey. I have not held that opinion since the decision against it."

The Congregation, having so far carried out the Pope's decree, dismissed him to his place:

"Et cum nihil aliud posset haberi in executionem decreti, habita ejus subscriptione, remissus fuit ad locum suum."

The next day he was summoned to the convent of the Minerva; and there, in the presence of the Cardinals and prelates of the Holy Office, the sentence we have already considered was pronounced, and he made his abjuration.

It appears that on the 30th of June his Holiness again expressly enjoined the publication of the sentence.[*]

The assertion, then, that the Pope directed the proceedings simply as a *doctor privatus*, and did not make himself officially responsible for the result, is plainly at variance with the truth. And whatever may be thought of the decree of the 16th of June as a display of personal feeling, its doctrinal significance is indisputable.

It was an act whereby his Holiness caused a Pontifical Congregation to inculcate it first on Galileo, and then on the Church, that the opinion of the earth's motion, having been absolutely condemned as false and altogether opposed to God's Word, ought to be detested by Catholics as a heresy opposed to the Holy Catholic and Apostolic Roman Church.

"In a thousand different ways," says Dr. Ward, "he (the Pope) may sufficiently indicate his intention of teaching the Church; but *whenever* and *however* he may do so*, the Holy Ghost interposes to preserve his instructions from every the slightest intermixture of error" (*Brief Summary*, p. 13). And elsewhere, drawing a parallel between the Pope and an Apostle, he says, "In the Christian Church there is no 'acceptation of persons;' no doctrinal favouritism: whatever doctrine is infallibly revealed *at all*, is infallibly revealed *for the*

---

[*] Ms. 30 Jun. 1633. *Les Pièces du Procès*, p. 95; and Gherardi's documents, see Appendix E.

whole Church. The Apostle may have originally addressed it to a local church, or *even to an individual;* but he none the less delivered it in his capacity of Universal Teacher. Still, then, we have come to no point of difference between the Apostolic Rule of Faith as understood by all Christians, and the modern Roman Catholic Rule as understood by Roman Catholics; except, indeed, that in the former there were twelve Universal Teachers, and in the latter there is no more than one" (*Second Letter to F. Ryder,* p. 32).

"The question is not about addressing himself, but about commanding interior assent. *But the Pope*—mark this—*never exacts absolute and unreserved assent to any doctrine from individual Catholics, except where he exacts such assent from the whole body of Christians, otherwise he would himself destroy that unity of faith which it is his office to maintain* " ("Infallibility and the Council," *Dublin Review,* Jan. 1870, p. 200). But Urban VIII. did exact from Galileo absolute and unreserved assent to the doctrine of the decision of 1616, therefore he exacted such assent from the whole body of Christians; therefore, it would seem, his Act was ex cathedrâ.

But I hear M. Bouix still pressing his objection:— "Granting," he says, "that the records you cite prove that his Holiness was in the front of the proceedings against Galileo, that he was fully responsible for the enforced abjuration of the doctrine of the earth's motion as a heresy, that he expressly ordered the Inquisitorial sentence wherein that doctrine was pronounced false, contrary to Scripture, and a heresy, to be published; nevertheless I contend that the Pope's acts in the matter were not his, as a *persona publica,* because they took place, so to say, behind the scenes, and were not officially notified to the Church. What I demand is some Bull, Brief, Apostolic Letter, or even a clause from the secretary of a Congregation, certifying that any Pope confirmed the condemnation of Galileo and the Copernican system. Such a thing does not exist, and to say that it does, is to say what is demonstrably false.

" Nulla producitur Bulla, nullum Breve, nullæ demum
Pontificiæ litteræ, quibus aut Paulus V. aut Urbanus VIII.,
aut alius quilibet Pontifex, dictam condemnationem Copernicani systematis ratam habuerit ac confirmaverit." " Quæstio est num Galilæi et Copernicani systematis condemnationem suam fecerit aliquis Romanus Pontifex per litteras
Apostolicas, vel per *solitam clausulam et publicam* attestationem de ipsius confirmatione aut speciali mandato. Id
a nullo Papa peractum dicimus, nec contrarium probant
objecta verba."

" Unde qui assereret Romanum Pontificem suam fecisse dictam condemnationem, id falso assereret, cum
nullum documentum id testetur, et non possent deesse
documenta, si revera res contigisset" (p. 473).

M. Bouix feels sure that he has, at last, made himself
quite safe. His requirements effectually estop all un-
pleasant evidence from unofficially published documents,
and he is so certain that his challenge cannot be met, that
he will stake his case on the issue.

Now I request the reader to note the tactics of this
controversialist. In his work *De Curia Romana*, when
he was dealing with the general question, and had not
before him this case of Galileo, the sole condition he laid
down as necessary and sufficient to make a decision Papal
and infallible, was that the Pope himself should have
decided the question. The only reason he gave for not
accounting Congregational decrees published without the
Pope's confirmation infallibly true was, that they are not
really Papal judgments at all, that the Pope's gift of
infallibility is strictly personal and incommunicable. But
in this his more recent work, *De Papa*, having to face
the objection to his doctrine supplied by the condemnation of Copernicanism, and finding himself unable to deny
that the judgment was really Papal, he shifts his position,
and now tells us, for a decision to be Papal and infallible,
the Pope must not only confirm the judgment, but the
fact that he has done so must be officially notified to
the Church by Bull, Brief, Apostolic Letter, or clause. I
am quite prepared to meet M. Bouix on his new ground,

but I think it well to call attention to the fact that it is new ground.

M. Bouix requires me to adduce some officially published document attesting the Pope's confirmation of the anti-Copernican decrees. The last thing he expected to see was a Bull to this effect. Nevertheless there is one.[*] Towards the end of his Pontificate, it occurred to Alexander VII. that it was his duty, as guardian of the household of Israel, to compose and place before the faithful a new Index of prohibited books that should be complete up to his time, and be more conveniently arranged than former indices. Whereupon he set to work with a specially chosen number of Cardinals; and in the March of 1664 there issued from the Vatican press a book entitled *Index Librorum prohibitorum Alexandri VII. Pontificis Maximi jussu editus.* It was prefaced by a Bull wherein the Pope describes the composition of his Index, and gives reasons for putting it forth. Amongst other things, the Pontiff says that the books noted therein will not be found distributed into three classes as they were in the Tridentine Index. That method of arrangement has been found inconvenient, and has given rise to mistaken estimates of the relatively bad character of the books prohibited. Yet it is so far retained that the class to which each book belongs will be found cited where the book is named, and also the decree by which the book was originally prohibited, in order that the whole history of each case may be known. "For this purpose," pursues the Pontiff, "we have caused the Tridentine and Clementine Indices to be added to this general Index, *and also all the relevant decrees up to the present time, that have been issued since the Index of our predecessor Clement,* that nothing profitable to the faithful interested in such matters might seem omitted. Since then all these directions have been faithfully and accurately carried out, and a general

---

[*] Until I drew attention to the matter in 1870, the bearing of this Papal Act on the case before us had, strange to say, been overlooked. Since then, attempts have been made to minimise its force. Unfortunately for the Ultramontanist, the very least the Bull can be fairly taken to mean is fatal to principles he is pledged to defend : see Introduction, pp. 14-17 ; and infra.

Index of this kind has been composed,—to which also the
rules of the Tridentine Index, with the observations and
instructions added to the Clementine Index, have been
prefixed; this same general Index as it is put forth,
composed by our order, revised, and printed at the press
of our Apostolic Camera, *and which we will should be
considered as though it were inserted in these presents,
together with all, and singular, the things contained therein,*
we, having taken the advice of our Cardinals, confirm,
and approve with Apostolic authority by the tenor of
these presents, and command and enjoin all persons
everywhere to yield this Index a constant and complete
obedience."

Turning to this Index, we find among the decrees the
Pope caused to be added thereto, the following: the "Quia
ad notitiam" of 1616; the "monitum" of 1620, declaring
the principles advocated by Copernicus on the position and
movement of the earth to be "repugnant to Scripture and
to its true and catholic interpretation;" the edict signed
by Bellarmine prohibiting and condemning Kepler's *Epi-
tome Astronomiæ Copernicanæ;* the edict of August 10th,
1684, prohibiting and condemning the *Dialogo di Galileo
Galilei;* and under the head "Libri," we find: "Libri
omnes docentes mobilitatem terræ, et immobilitatem solis,
in decr. 5 Martii, 1616." These, therefore, were some
of the things the Pope confirmed and approved with Apostolic authority by the tenor of his Bull. It is clear, therefore, that the condemnation of Copernicanism was ratified
and approved by the Pope himself, not merely behind the
scenes, but publicly in the face of the whole Church, by
the authority of a Bull addressed to all the faithful.
Nay, more—and I call particular attention to this point—
the Index to which the decrees in question were attached,
was confirmed and approved by the Pope, not as a thing
external to the Bull, but as though actually in it, "quem
præsentibus nostris pro inserto haberi volumus;" and
therefore it, and all it contained, came to the Church
directly from the Pope himself, speaking to her as her
Head, "as guardian of the household of Israel, as the

shepherd who had to take care of the Lord's flock, to protect it from the evils that threatened it, to see that the sheep redeemed by the precious blood of the Saviour were not led astray from the path of truth."

It cannot, then, be said with truth that the Bull in question confirmed the decrees simply as Congregational edicts, and left them in the category in which it found them.* Congregational decisions that are taken up by the Pope as Head of the Church, and are presented by him in that capacity to the faithful with an assurance that he approves and confirms them with Apostolic authority, obviously must, by the very fact of being so conditioned, possess the precise warrant to be accounted ex cathedra, the lack of which is the main reason for disputing the ex cathedra claims of Congregational decrees issued under ordinary circumstances; that is, they come to the Church directly from the Pope himself acting as her Head, whereas the latter come to the Church only indirectly from the Pope, through the medium of his delegates.

In the following year another Index was published by the Pope's order. It is a small volume, containing the rules of the Tridentine Index, a preface by F. Vincentius Fanus, Secretary of the Congregation, and the list of prohibited books, with the names of the authors; but the prohibition under the head "Libri" is noteworthy : "Libri omnes, et quicunque libelli, commentarii, compositiones, consulta, epistolæ, glossæ, opuscula, orationes, responsa, tractatus, tam typis editi, *quam manuscripti*, continentes et tractantes infrascriptas materias, seu de infrascriptis materiis. . . . . De mobilitate terræ, et immobilitate solis." Nevertheless, Dr. Ward, as we shall see, would have us believe that the Church "fully permitted the publication of every discoverable scientific objection to geocentricism"!

I have yet another question to raise. If the Ultramontanist could show us that the judgment against

---

* I allude to what Professor Grisar has recently asserted on the subject. See his work, *Historisch-Theologische Untersuchungen über die Urtheile der Römischen Congregationen im Galileiprocess*, p. 161.

Copernicus was nothing more than a decision on a matter
of doctrine put forth by a Pontifical Congregation, would
he be out of his difficulties? I think not. He is obliged
by his theory to regard the Munich Brief as an infallible
utterance. Accordingly, he must accept as true an instruc-
tion to this effect. "It results from the principles of true
theology that men cannot have that perfect adhesion to
revealed truth which is necessary for the progress of
science and the refuting of error, unless (1) they yield
that subjection which is to be rendered in an act of divine
faith, not only to dogmata expressly defined by decrees
of Œcumenical Councils and the Roman Pontiffs, but also
to those things which are delivered as divinely revealed
by the teaching authority of the Church dispersed
throughout the world, and which are therefore accounted
by Catholic theologians to appertain to the faith. And
unless (2) they subject themselves in conscience as well
to the decisions on matters pertaining to doctrine that
are put forth by the Pontifical Congregations; as also to
those heads of doctrine that are retained by the common
and consistent consent of Catholics as theological truths,
and conclusions so certain that opinions adverse to the
same, though not to be called heretical, yet deserve some
other censure."

Now, here the Pope apparently bids us attribute the
same authority to decisions on matters of doctrine that
emanate from the Pontifical Congregations, as to those
heads of doctrine Catholics are bound to account theologically certain. In other words, he seems to claim for
the former theological certainty. But not to press this
point, and taking the words of the Brief as they stand,
we must conclude from them, that Catholic men of science
who lived at the end of the seventeenth century were
bound in conscience not to welcome, but to discredit, the
recent announcement of the law of gravitation; that
Newton, from a Christian point of view, acted wrongly in
writing, and still more in publishing, his *Principia*; that
he ought, from the first, to have recognised that his hypothesis was contrary to Scripture, and therefore incapable

of verification; and since the anti-Copernican decrees were
in force after Richer's and Bradley's discoveries, it would
seem that Catholic men of science may find themselves in
the predicament of having to submit to decisions that
are almost demonstrably false.

Thus, the case before us does a great deal more than
exemplify the truth that Pontifical Congregations are not,
strictly speaking, infallible. It shows that they can make
mistakes we should not expect from learned and prudent
men. It demonstrates that God will permit their maturely
formed, repeatedly expressed, and long-sustained judgment to be in direct antagonism to the truth He is dis-
closing through "the light that lighteth every man that
cometh into the world." How, then, can any dominion
over the scientific thought of their age be legitimately
claimed for them? Here Dr. Ward comes to the rescue,
and with characteristic boldness denies that their condemnation of Copernicanism was a mistake at all in any
proper sense of the term. He explains himself thus:

"If a decree is put forth claiming infallibility, it purports to have God's unfailing guarantee of its truth. But
it is most certain that Galileo's condemnation was *not*
put forth with any claim to infallibility; and we ask,
therefore, what such a decree *does* purport to be? No
answer but one can possibly be given, as a moment's
consideration will evince. It purports to instruct Catholics
in that conclusion which legitimately follows from existing
data. Now, we argued at much length, that the con-
trariety of Copernicanism to Scripture *was* the consequence
legitimately resulting from the data of 1616 (see pp.
140-152; 160; 182). The reason why Copernicanism is
now justly held to be consistent with Scripture is its
having been scientifically established (pp. 142-3); but so
far was this from having been the case in Galileo's time,
that, on the contrary, as a matter of mere science, its
falsehood was more probable than its truth (pp. 146-152).
Nor was Galileo's confidence in the scientific strength of
his theory any presumption of its real strength, because
the one main argument on which he laid his stress is now

admitted by every one to have been absolutely worthless (p. 400). By accident he was right; but, 'formally,' even as a man of science, he was wrong.

" The decree purported to be—not infallibly guaranteed by God, but—the true conclusion from existing data. Well, it *was* the true conclusion from existing data: how, therefore, in any true sense, can it be called mistaken? On the contrary, it afforded 'true doctrinal guidance to contemporary Catholics' (p. 186). For (1) it inculcated on them that doctrinal lesson which legitimately resulted from existing data; and (2) it warned them against 'a most false, proud, irreverent, and dangerous principle of Scriptural interpretation.' What is that principle? ' The contradicting the obvious and traditional sense of Scripture, on the strength of a theory scientifically unlikely.' And this is a principle as anti-Catholic now as it was then "* (*Doctrin. Decis.* pp. 199, 200).

This account of the matter, besides that it utterly fails to do justice to the terms of the condemnation—*false* and *altogether* opposed to the divine Scripture—lies open to this fatal objection: Its interpretation of the decree is the one Urban VIII. and his Congregation pro-

---

* It is worth observing, that Foscarinus, whose position the Congregation singled out to exemplify what it meant to condemn, takes the greatest pains to guard against giving the slightest countenance to such a principle. He insists *in limine* on the scientific merit of the heliocentric theory, and makes its acknowledged likelihood a reason for attempting its theological defence: " Perciò molti moderni si sono indotti e persuasi finalmente a sequirlo, ma con alquanto di timore e di rimorso ; perciocchè parve a loro, che alla Scrittura Sacra ei fusse talmente contrario, che non si potessero con esso conciliare le autorità, che gli repugnavano. . . . Io per me, considerate tutte queste cose (per il desiderio, che tengo, che le dottrine ricevano quant' è possibile aumento, lume e perfezione, e se ne sgombrino tutti gli errori, con rilucervi dentro la pura verità), sono andato fra me stesso speculando in questo modo. O questa opinione de' Pittagorici è vera, o no ; se non è vera, non è degna che se ne parli, ne che si metta in campo ; se è vera, poco importa che contraddica a tutti i filosofi ed astronomi del mondo, e che per sequirla e praticarla s' abbia da fare una nuova filosofia ed astronomia, dependente da nuovi principj ed ipotesi, che questa pone. Quello, che appartiene alle Scritture Sacre, nè anco gli nuocerà, perciocchè una verità non è contraria all' altra. Se dunque è vera l' opinione Pittagorica, senza dubbio Iddio avrà talmente dettate le parole della Scrittura Sacra che possano ricevere senso accomodato a quell' opinione, e conciliamento con esse. Questo è il motivo, che m' indusse a considerare ed a cercare, (*stante la probabilità evidente della già detta*

hibited: "Tratta la cosa come non decisa, e come che si aspetti e non si presupponga la definizione."

If Rome meant what she said, either in 1633 she utterly mistook the force and scope of her own decree issued about seventeen years before, in which case she blundered over the very easiest matter that could possibly come before her; or that decree was meant to be taken as absolutely true, in which case even Dr. Ward must admit that it was a mistake in every sense of the term.

The truth is, Dr. Ward proceeds throughout on misconceptions of fact. To begin with, he supposes (pp. 157 and 172) that there were two decrees of the Index in 1616, issued about the same time; one purely doctrinal, the other purely disciplinary. The former, he holds, was the declaration referred to in Bellarmine's certificate; the latter was the "Quia etiam ad notitiam." The former, he says, certainly affected liberty of thought; but then it was never repeated, and concerned only contemporary Catholics. And he bids us notice (p. 183) how it avoided the dangerous and untheological confusion implied in censuring Copernicanism as *false*. The latter, he admits, continued in force to the time of Benedict XIV., and must be considered for all practical purposes to have been reenacted by every successive intermediate Pontiff; but then, being purely disciplinary, it affected only liberty of action.

The reader knows that the purely doctrinal and tem-

---

opinione) il modo, e la strada di accordare molti luoghi della Scrittura Sacra con essa, ed interpretrali, non senza fondamenti teologici e fisici, in modo tale che non gli contraddicano affatto; acciò quando ella si vedrà (per caso) e determinata espressamente, e con certezza esser vera, (*siccome ora per probabile è ricevuta*) non se gli ritrovi intoppo alcuno, che l' impedisca e che gli dia fastidio, privando indegnamente il mondo del venerabile e sacrosanto commercio della tanto da tutti i buoni desiderata verità " (Lettera del P. Foscarini, *Opere di G. G.* vol. v. pp. 460-1).

The real question at issue was, are the expressions of the sacred writers in relation to the physical order to be judged by the same rule as those relating to things moral and spiritual. In condemning Copernicanism as altogether contrary to Scripture, Rome virtually said yes. Was that the right answer?

porary decree, Dr. Ward says was never repeated, never existed; that the decree Dr. Ward would persuade us was a purely disciplinary enactment, Rome ruled to be doctrinal as well as disciplinary; that the dangerous and untheological confusion Dr. Ward would relegate to an unauthoritative preamble, Rome indorsed and insisted on as a part of the declaration.

"Et ut prorsus tolleretur tam perniciosa doctrina, neque ulterius serperet in grave detrimentum Catholicæ veritatis, emanavit decretum a Sacra Congregatione Indicis, quo fuerunt prohibiti libri qui tractant de hujusmodi doctrina, et ea declarata fuit falsa, et omnino contraria sacræ et divinæ Scripturæ."

One would not have supposed it possible for a man of Dr. Ward's ability, with this passage and its context—not to speak of other evidence—before him, to miss seeing what Bellarmine meant. But I observe that, after professing to have compared Dr. Madden's translation of it with the Latin, he retains and founds his argument on a word in the former that does not exist in the latter.

Speaking of the sentence in p. 163, he says: "We will draw special attention to a few passages by italics. The translation is founded on Dr. Madden's; but we have made various changes, to bring it (as we think) into nearer accordance with the Latin." Now mark how he translates and italicises the extract just given: "And in order that so pernicious a doctrine should be taken wholly away, and no longer allowed to spread, to the great detriment of the Catholic Truth, a decree emanated *from the Sacred College of the Index*, in which the books were prohibited which treat of doctrine of this kind; and that doctrine was declared false by *it*, and altogether contrary to the sacred and divine Scriptures."

And how the interpolated "*it*" is utilised in p. 169:

"All their expressions, however, are quite inconsistent with the supposition, that they regarded this decree as the Pope's judgment ex cathedrâ. *They ascribe that decree, in fact, to the Congregation of the Index, and not to the Pope.*"

Again, look at the considerations which constitute Dr. Ward's proof that the heliocentric theory at the time of its condemnation was scientifically unlikely.

He begins (p. 146) by insisting on the proposition that simplicity is no proof of truth; and gives us the benefit of Mr. Mill's remark on the subject. He asserts, " that in Copernicus' or even Galileo's time, this argument hardly furnished a presumption, much less did it establish a likelihood" (p. 147).

Then, to show that " before Galileo's time the Copernican theory was a mere guess, a mere conjecture," he quotes from De Morgan's *Motion of the Earth* a specimen of what he calls " the chief," but what the Professor calls " the more common arguments," then used on both sides; and exclaims, " Such were the arguments of which it has been gravely contended that they would justify Catholics in disbelieving the obvious and traditional sense of God's written Word !" (p. 149.)

But when those arguments were most in vogue the Copernican interpretation of Scripture was *not* prohibited, and we may safely say, never would have been, if better ones had not been adduced. So that one does not see how their absurdity helps Dr. Ward.

We are next presented with the following account of the scientific status of Copernicanism in Galileo's time, from what Dr. Ward calls an extremely fair and able paper in the *Rambler* of January 1852.*

* The following is Delambre's summary : " Les réflexions de Copernic, de Képler, et de Galilée suffisaient pour qu'on fût Copernicien de bonne foi, de persuasion et d'inclination ; *on voyoit une foule de probabilités ;* les adversaires mêmes conviennent que pour les tables astronomiques l'hypothèse est plus commode, et ils la permettent en ce sens. Galilée, par ses découvertes, a levé quelques difficultés ; les phases de Vénus et la mesure plus exacte des diamètres, la rotation du Soleil, les satellites de Jupiter, ont augmenté des probabilités *déjà si fortes.* Les lois de Képler ont ajouté à la beauté et à la simplicité du système. Newton en montrant que les lois de Képler sont des corollaires mathématiques du principe de la pesanteur universelle, a lié plus intimement encore toutes les parties du système ; il a prouvé l'impossibilité physique du mouvement du Soleil autour de la Terre : l'expérience de Richer prouve le mouvement diurne ; l'aberration découverte par Bradley démontre le mouvement annuel. La question est irrévocablement décidée. Toutes les objections *assez futiles d'ailleurs,* disparaissent devant des preuves si positives et si bien liées. Les théologiens sensés seront les premiers aujourd'hui

H

"The Ptolemaic theory had sufficed for centuries to explain and to account for all the observed motions of the planets as logically and as precisely as the Copernican theory does now; and it was during all this time found capable of taking in and preserving all the exact knowledge of the world. Such being the state of the case . . . . . a new system suddenly makes its appearance, and claims to supersede the old; and on what grounds? Because it accounted for phenomena in a more simple way than the old theory. But then the old theory *did* account for phenomena, however complex it might have been; and *simplicity is not always an infallible test of truth.* Again, it was in analogy with the newly-discovered system of Jupiter's satellites, and accounted for the moon-like phases of Venus which the telescope revealed. *And these three points constituted about the whole proof which Galileo could bring forward.* His other arguments, from the tides and magnetism of the earth, are all moonshine. The Newtonian theory of gravitation was then unknown; and the periods of the revolutions of the planets appeared quite as disconnected and random as did the cycles and epicycles of the old theory. Newton first explained the one law on which the revolutions depended; before his time *there was nothing to make the Copernican system more plausible and reasonable than the Ptolemaic theory. The modern demonstrations of the annual motion of the earth—* namely, the micrometrical observations on the discs of the bodies of the solar system, and especially the great discovery of the aberration of light, by which that motion is made evident to the senses—*were then unknown :* and as to the diurnal motion, it was unproved till Richer's

---

à demander qu'on interprète l'Ecriture comme le proposaient Képler Ga-lilée et Foscarini.

"Riccioli avoue que les inquisiteurs n'ont prononcé sur le sens des passages de l'Ecriture que d'après le témoignage des astronomes d'alors, qui ne voyaient aucune démonstration valable du mouvement de la Terre. *Enfin, quand on compare les éloges que Riccioli donne à l'hypothèse qu'il combat, à la faiblesse des raisons qu'il lui oppose, on croit voir un avocat chargé malgré lui de plaider une cause qu'il sait mauvaise, qui n'apporte que des arguments pitoyables, parce qu'il n'y en a pas d'autres, et qui sait lui-même que sa cause est perdue*" (Delambre, *Ast. Mod.* vol. i. p. 680).

voyage to Cayenne, where he was obliged to shorten his pendulum. And it is only within the last few months that an experiment has been devised by which this motion may be exhibited to the senses—namely, by the apparent revolution of the plane of the vibration of a pendulum fixed over a horizontal table. *Before these demonstrations, there was no solid reason to induce men to disbelieve the evidence of their senses. The most decided Copernicans were reduced to mere probabilities,* and were obliged to confine themselves to preaching up the simplicity of the Copernican system, as compared with the absurd complexity of that of Ptolemy. It is now generally taken for granted that the Copernican theory is self-evident. So far from that being the case, we may safely affirm, that *up to Galileo's* time the balance of proof *was in favour of the old system;* that is, the old system was at that time *the* probable one, and Copernicus' theory the improbable one " (pp. 15, 16).

This writer is not famous for his caution ; yet even he does not venture to commit himself to the position that in Galileo's time, *i.e. when the doctrine of the earth's motion was condemned,* the balance of proof was in favour of the geocentric theory. Accordingly Dr. Ward supplements him as follows :

" But fairly and temperately as this writer expresses himself, it would seem nevertheless that he states Galileo's scientific status at somewhat greater advantage than truth will warrant. M. Artaud, in the volume named at the head of this article (pp. 306-321), draws attention to a paper contributed by M. Léon Desdouits, a Catholic savant, to the *Univers Catholique* of March 1841. The *gravity of the air,* M. Desdouits reminds his reader, was first discovered by Torricelli after Galileo's death. The Florentine philosopher therefore, from ignorance of this fundamental truth, was in an inextricable difficulty. To say that the earth is whirled through the terrestrial air, was plainly inconsistent with phenomena ; while yet he could give no sufficient reason for supposing that the earth carries the air with it in its revolution. He was unable therefore to complete a theory of his own which he could even reconcile with known facts; and since his opponents had no difficulty whatever in so reconciling theirs, it is not too much to say that his hypothesis, in its then incomplete state, was 'scientifically unlikely,' *i.e.* that there were stronger grounds for rejecting than for accepting it."

Here is a pretty piece of confusion! *What weight* the air has was not accurately known in Galileo's time; nor till Torricelli's experiment in 1643 had any proof been given that the pressure of the atmosphere causes the phenomena of a common pump.* But the following extract from Baliani's letter to Galileo, dated October 26, 1630,† will show the sort of reminder those need who talk of Torricelli as the discoverer of the gravity of the air, and argue that his master must have been placed in an inextricable difficulty from ignorance of this fundamental truth. I give Mr. Drinkwater's translation :

"I have believed that a vacuum may exist naturally ever since I knew *that the air has sensible weight, and that you taught me in one of your letters how to find its weight exactly*, though I have not yet succeeded with that experiment. From that moment I took up the notion that it is not repugnant to the nature of things that there should be a vacuum, but merely that it is difficult to produce. To explain myself more clearly : *if we allow that the air has weight, there is no difference between air and water except in degree.* At the bottom of the sea the weight of the water above me compresses everything round my body; and it strikes me that the same thing must happen in the air, we being placed at the bottom of its immensity. We do not

* Yet *the hypothesis* was not new; for, to quote Dr. Whewell, "Descartes, in a letter of the date of 1631, explains the suspension of mercury in a tube closed at the top, by the pressure of the column of air reaching to the clouds" (*History of Ind. Sciences*, vol. ii. p. 52). Even Aristotle knew that the air has weight (cf. *De Cœlo*, lib. iv. c. iv.).

† *Opere di G. G.* Fl. ed. vol. ix. p. 211.

feel its weight, nor the compression round us, because our bodies are made capable of supporting it. But if we were in a vacuum, then the weight of the air above our heads would be felt. It would be felt very great, but not infinite, and therefore determinable; and it might be overcome by a force proportioned to it. In fact I estimate it to be such, that to make a vacuum I believe we require a force greater than that of a column of water thirty feet high." [*]

As to the summary from the *Rambler*, its accuracy may be estimated by its assertion that "before Newton's time there was nothing to make the Copernican system more plausible and reasonable than the Ptolemaic." Long before Newton's time the ablest anti-Copernicans had abandoned the *Ptolemaic* theory as quite indefensible.[†] Kepler's and Galileo's discoveries left but two types of system for the scientific man to choose between—the Copernican and the Tychonic. It was not, as the *Rambler* puts it, the case of an upstart theory trying to supersede one that had been in possession for ages, and which was fully up to its work; but of a struggle between two new systems,—the Copernican having the advantage in point of age,—for the place left vacant by one that had received its deathblow from both. And their claims may be fairly stated thus:—Both could account for the celestial phenomena—the latter nearly or quite as well as the former; but the former was by far the simpler explanation, and as an hypothesis was universally preferred. And when it was known that the planets were

---

[*] *Life of Galileo*, p. 90.

[†] " Tra questi si può comprendere il Padre Clavio Gesuita, uomo dottissimo, il quale vedendo il poco fondamento dell' opinione comune, quantunque egli per altro confuti la Pittagorica, nondimeno confessa che gli astronomi, per levare molte difficoltà, che non pienamente sono tolte dal comune sistema, sono sforzati a cercare di provvedersene di alcun altro " (Lettera del P. Foscarini, *G. G. Opere*, vol. v. p. 460).

" Omnes denique planetas solem motu proprio circumcurrere. Verum universa hæc et plura ejusdem novæ cœlestis philosophiæ volentes concedimus " (Fromundus, *Ant. Arist*. c. xvii. p. 91).

Conf. Riccioli, *Astr. Refor.* vol. i. p. 85, and proleg. viii. 9.

" Utra hypothesis Copernici an Brahei (*nam antiquas Ptolemaicas falsas esse certum est*) sequenda sit " (J. Kep. Admonitio; Venturi, vol. ii. p. 74). And conf. Gassendi, tom. i. 134.

globular opaque bodies, like the earth deriving light from the sun, and that they moved round the sun; and when it seemed to be the law that the smaller body should revolve round the larger,* the *onus probandi* lay very decidedly with the advocates of the more complex arrangement giving the earth an apparently abnormal position.

Now there never had been more than two good arguments on their side—one against the diurnal, and one against the annual, movement of the earth. Tycho had urged, if the earth revolves on its axis once in twenty-four hours, how is it that a piece of lead dropped from a high tower falls straight to the base, instead of being left behind? And if the earth moves round the sun once in the year, how is it that the fixed stars present no annual parallax, in spite of the enormous dimensions of the earth's orbit, and yet some of them have a diameter of two minutes?

Galileo announced, and verified by experiment, the law that meets the first objection. The second was shown by the telescope† to derive its force from an optical delusion. Besides, in its best days it was fairly cancelled by a counter one from the Copernican side. The great size which the assertion of the earth's annual motion seemed to require for the fixed stars was no harder to believe, than the prodigious velocity we attribute to the heavenly bodies in denying the diurnal rotation.

* Credibilius enim est, magnum esse corpus, circa quod minora circumeunt: sic enim Saturnus, Jupiter, Mars, Venus, Mercurius omnia minora sunt corpora ipso corpore Solis, circa quod illa circumeunt: sic Luna minor est Tellure, circa quam Luna circumit; sic quatuor satellites Joviales minores sunt ipso Jovis corpore, circa quod illi volvuntur. Jam vero si Sol movetur, Sol maximus et tres superiores, omnes terra majores, circa tellurem minorem circumibunt; credibilius igitur est, Tellurem, corpus parvum, circa Solis corpus magnum circumire " (Kepler, *As. Cop.* lib. iv. p. 544).

"When," says Dr. Whewell, "the system of the planet Jupiter offered to the bodily eye a model or image of the solar system according to the views of Copernicus, it supported the belief of such an arrangement of the planets by an analogy all but irresistible. It thus, as a writer of our own times—Sir J. Herschel—has said, 'gave the holding turn to the opinions of mankind respecting the Copernican system ' " (*Hist. of Ind. Sciences*, vol. i. p. 301).

† " Periti artifices negant, ullam quantitatem veluti rotundi corporis detegi per inspectionem telescopii, quin potius quo perfectius instrumentum hoc magis fixas representari ut puncta mera, ex quibus radii lucidi in speciem crinium exeant disperganturque " (Kepler, *Ep. As. Cop.* lib. iv. p. 498).

The physical difficulties Dr. Ward insists on, Tycho himself discredited;[*] and it is obvious that they could not have given a moment's trouble to any one possessing the knowledge Baliani's letter implies.

Copernicanism, then, was condemned when its formal superiority was universally admitted, when it was supported by a powerful argument from analogy, and had no greater difficulties to contend with than its rival; and as no one in his senses will say that a theory in such a position deserves to be called scientifically unlikely,— *false* was the term used,—we may safely pronounce the attempt to justify the decision by an appeal to the scientific data of the time an egregious failure.

Dr. Ward thinks very highly of the scriptural argument for the judgment, and is amazed that Dr. Pusey should speak of the mistakes of theologians in the matter. Yet he himself gives up all the passages on which those theologians, in fact, mainly took their stand; and admits " that perhaps it may be truly maintained with regard to all those texts which speak of the sun's motion, that they merely purport to describe phenomena as such, and that in their simple and obvious sense they would not be otherwise understood." But he bids us consider the following: " (Ps. ciii. 5) ' Thou who didst found the earth on its stable support (super stabilitatem suam); *it shall not be moved for ever.*' (Ps. xcii. 1) ' He hath fixed the earth, *which shall not be moved.*'[†] Job xxxviii. 4-6, where God Himself speaks, ' Where wast thou,' asks the Creator, ' when *I laid the foundation of the earth ?* Upon what *were its supports established ?* (Super quo bases illius stabilitæ sunt ?)' Texts similar are Ps. xvii. 16, lxxxi. 5,

---

[*] " Nec tot inconvenientia hinc proveniunt quot plerique arbitrantur; quæque in Poemate Sphærico clarissimi illius poetæ Buchanani Scoti, mei, cum in vivis esset, amici eximii, nuper publicata sunt, locum hic non habent. Is enim non animadvertit posito motu terreno, mare et circumfluum proximumque aerem una pari concitatione convolvi, ideoque nullam violentiam causari, nec absurditatem, quantam in omnibus iis, quæ in contrarium adducit, provenire " (Tycho Brahé, *Epist. Astr.* p. 74).

[†] The mere expression, " non commovebitur " (Ps. xcii. 2), Bishop Wilkins remarked, proves nothing ; for the Hebrew is radically the same in these : " Perfice gressus meos in semitis tuis, ut non moveantur vestigia mea " (Ps. xvi. 5) ; " Non det in commotionem pedem tuum " (Ps. cxx. 3) ; and Ps. xv. 8.

xcv. 10, cxxxv. 6 ; Prov. iii. 19, viii. 29. We entreat our
readers to study successively these various texts. It is
most unfair to speak, as Dr. Pusey speaks, of the mistakes
of theologians in the interpretation of these texts. Surely,
had it not been for the Copernican theory, no one, who
believes in the inspiration of Scripture, would have
thought of doubting, that in them God expressly declares
the earth's immobility. If any one hesitates at this
statement on first reading them, he must be convinced, if
he will put into words his own version of their meaning.
Take, *e.g.*, the first: Ps. ciii. 5:* ' Thou who didst found
the earth on its stable support ; it shall not be moved for
ever.' This means, as we are now aware, 'Thou who
didst place the earth in its orbit; it shall not cease from
steadily revolving therein.' But who will say that this
is a sense in the slightest degree obvious ? And the
same test may be applied with equal efficacy to every
text we have named " (*Auth. of Doc. Dec.* pp. 141, 142).

Yet surely in a book that we admit may naturally
speak of the sun as moving, and describe it as "a bride-
groom coming out of his bridechamber;" "rejoicing as a
giant to run the way;"—"his going out is from the end
of heaven, and his circuit even to the end thereof,"—we
need not be surprised to find the earth depicted under
images of things fixed and stable.

The obvious earth of the Bible is, no doubt, an immovable earth; but then *it is also the immovable earth of
common observation, of a much ruder conception of things
even than the Ptolemaic.* It rests on stable supports, on
foundations placed none can tell where; and the movement denied is that of a building falling to ruin through
the shaking or slipping of its basis.

Test the following by Dr. Ward's rule: (Job xxxvii. 18)
"Tu forsitan cum eo fabricatus es *cœlos, qui solidissimi
quasi œre fusi sunt ?"* (Job xxvi. 11) "*Columnæ cœli* con-
tremiscunt et pavent ad nutum ejus." (Ps. cxxxv. 6)
" Qui firmavit terram *super aquas.*" (Ps. xxiii. 2) "Ipse

* Dr. Ward is most unfortunate in his choice. The Vulgate is "*non
inclinabitur.*"

super maria fundavit eum, et *super flumina* præparavit eum." (Job xxxviii. 8-11) " Quis *conclusit ostiis mare*, quando erumpebat quasi de vulva procedens ; cum ponerem nubem vestimentum ejus, et caligine illud quasi pannis infantiæ obvolverem? Circumdedi illud terminis meis, et *posui vectem et ostia; et dixi, usque huc venies, et non procedes amplius; et hic confringes tumentes fluctus tuos.*" (Prov. viii. 26-29) "Adhuc terram non fecerat et flumina, *et cardines orbis terræ.* Quando præparabat cœlos aderam ; quando certa lege et gyro vallabat abyssos ; quando *æthera firmabat sursum,* et librabat fontes aquarum ; quando *circumdabat mari terminum suum, et legem ponebat aquis, ne transirent fines suos; quando appendebat fundamenta terræ.*" (Jer. v. 22) "Me ergo non timebitis, ait Dominus, et a facie mea non dolebitis? *qui posui arenam terminum mari, præceptum sempiternum, quod non præteribit, et commovebuntur, et non poterunt, et intumescent fluctus ejus, et non transibunt illud.*"

When men knew that the heavens were not a firm vault " most strong, as if they were of molten brass " " supported by pillars "; that the earth has " no foundations," " no bases," " no ends," is not " surrounded by water naturally tending to overflow it,"—theologians had received a pretty significant hint that the texts Dr. Ward refers to must not be pressed to mean more than the stability of the earth in its appointed order, whatever that may be. Surely it is indisputable that the course they adopted was more rash, more calculated to bring the authority of Scripture and the Church into contempt, than anything Foscarinus or Galileo wrote : "Mostrando con quanta circospezione bisogni andare intorno a quelle cognizioni naturali, che non sono *de fide,* alle quali possono arrivar l' esperienze e le dimostrazioni necessarie, e quanto perniciosa cosa sarebbe l' asserire come dottrina risoluta nelle sacre Scritture alcuna proposizione, della quale una volta si potesse avere dimostrazione in contrario " (*Letter to Monsignor Dini,* 16th February 1614).

Thirdly, in spite of the declaration that it was a most grave error to suppose that the opinion of the earth's

motion *could in any manner be probable*—in spite of Rome's
solemn judgment that Galileo's doctrine must be regarded
as false and heretical,—Dr. Ward would have us believe
(p. 182) that Catholics were not *prohibited from publishing
any scientific argument in behalf of Copernicanism*, and
that the ecclesiastical authorities *allowed consistently* (!)
*throughout the fullest and freest scientific discussion of the
theory.*

I presume he relies on the permission given to treat
Copernicanism *as an hypothesis.** If so, I venture to
remind him that an hypothesis may be held in two ways:
(1) as a possibly true explanation, for the purpose of
being tested; (2) as an *avowedly false one*, to facilitate the
conception of phenomena, and for convenience in making
calculations;† and that to tolerate an hypothesis only in
the latter sense excludes its scientific discussion.

Melchior Inchofer, the Consultor of the Holy Office,
ought to be a good authority on the matter. He says:

"Dico ... licere ex hypothesi assumpto motu terræ uti
ad putationes mathematicas conficiendas. Patet tum
ex consensu Ecclesiæ, quæ Copernicanæ putationis usum
permittit, etsi principia ex quibus illa deducitur *absolutè
damnet*. . . . . Porro in usu calculi Copernici duplex esse
potest progressus. Alter ex hypothesi pure mathematica,
quæ tamen a principiis veris et physicis etiam putatis,
minime censeatur pendere. Alter ex hypothesi, quæ
existimetur principiis naturalibus et veris, vel quæ talia
habentur niti, et ex eisdem conclusiones certas ac demon-
stratas, vel quæ tales reputantur, deducere.

"Juxta primum, licet eatenus operari, ut posito illo
systemate pleraque phænomena explicentur, periodique
omnes motuum, et quicquid huc spectare potest, arithmetice
et velut ex arte subducantur, non aliter quam si ex
positionibus Ptolemæi, aut quibusvis aliis præter Coper-
nicanas censerentur. Ceterum sicut mathematicus, si
postulet lineam dari infinitam, aut quavis quantitate continua majorem vel minorem, recte concludet superstrui

* See Appendix D.
† I respectfully call Mr. Arnold's attention to this distinction.

posse triangulum infinitum, neque tamen verum erit in
rerum natura dari lineam infinitam. Recte præterea
deducet lineam esse longitudinem sine latitudine et pro-
funditate, si punctum fluere, et lineam esse fluxum puncti
supponat, quod tamen reipsa falsum est et physice impossibile .... ita prorsus dato systemate Copernicano,
etsi falso et a ratione alieno, deduci possunt putationes
veræ, eademque principia vaga (ut hinc etiam falsitas
arguatur et incertitudo) applicari possunt ad. alia, quæ in
physicis genuinas habent causas. .... *At in systemate
Copernicano, progredi licet eatenus, ut examinari tantum
queat, an ex falsis illis positionibus, rectæ et cum syderiis
motibus cohærentes eliciantur supputationes.*

"Juxta alterum sensum, in usu calculi Copernici
eatenus est progrediendum, *ut nedum de principiis, nisi
ostendendo eorum falsitatem, sed neque de ipsa putatione
tanquam ex vera hypothesi pendente, liceat disputare:* Idque
tum ob rationes initio capitis adductas; tum quia puri
mathematici, si in plerisque aliis, in præsenti argumento
ad physicas atque etiam theologicas rationes reducto, non
discernunt, quid ex quo sequatur, necessitate vel conse-
quentiæ vel consequentis. Idcirco non solum paralogizant,
sed etiam inepta et falsa Scripturarum interpretatione
errant, aliisque periculum errandi creant. Ob quam, inter
alia, causam, recte cavit S. Congregatio Indicis ne quid
præter usum calculi Copernicani, circa hypotheses stabi-
liendos affirmaretur" (*Melch. Inchofer. Tractatus Syllepticus*,
pp. 48-50).

And Palaccus writes to the same effect: "Dicamus ergo
Eminentissimorum Cardinalium Congregationem non pro-
hibuisse terræ motum, *adeo ut nulli liceret cœli difficultates
exponere supposito terræ motu, dummodo is qui explicat clare
ostendat se non illa hypothesi ut vera niti, sed tantum ex falso
principio procedere ut rem melius aperiat,* eo fere modo quo
theologi plurima theologica explicant, dum aiunt, suppo-
namus Deum non esse Infinitum, vel Justum, et sic de
ceteris; vel quod idem est, si per impossibile Deus non
esset Infinitus, vel Justus, et cetera, id vel illud sequeretur" (*Anticopernicus Catholicus Assert.* ix. p. 5).

Plainly, the state ot the case was this : To use the distinction so clearly explained by Professor de Morgan,* a Catholic might argue as much as he pleased in behalf of *mathematical,* but not at all in behalf of *physical,* Copernicanism. That is, he might show that if the earth rotated on its axis and about the sun, the heavenly appearances would be as they are; and he might use the supposition of such movements for astronomical calculations; and he might, of course, point out the weakness of this or that anti-Copernican objection. But anything beyond this, any attempt to show that there were facts nothing but the earth's motion could explain ; anything, in short, that implied a belief that the reason why things appear as they would if the earth moved, is that it does move, was directly in defiance of Rome's decision, and, according to the judgment of 1633, constituted matter for prosecution on suspicion of heresy.

Lastly, Dr. Ward (p. 172) quietly takes for granted that the decision of 1633 was purely personal to Galileo, and concerned no one else. How completely at variance with the truth is this notion, we have already seen.

M. de l'Epinois' extracts have shown us that both before and after it was pronounced, the Pope himself expressly commanded the Congregation to publish the sentence, that all, and particularly those whose pursuits would bring them across the question at issue, might know how it had been decided. And from the same source we learn how thoroughly the order was obeyed.

The minutes of the process record letters acknowledging the receipt or publication of the sentence from Florence, Padua, Bologna, Naples, Venice, Ferrara, Vienna, Perugia, Como, Pavia, Milan, Cremona, Reggio, from the Nuncio Apostolic in France, from the Nuncio Apostolic at Brussels, from the Nuncio at Madrid, from the Rector of

---

* See " Notes on the Antegalilean Copernicans " (*Comp. to the Almanack* for 1855, pp. 1, 2): " Every person," remarks the professor, " who knows the heavenly motions as they appear before our eyes, and has a little knowledge of geometry, *must be a mathematical Copernican.* He cannot fail to see that a Copernican universe would show the same appearances as that in which he lives."

the University of Douai, and others (see *Les Pièces du Procès*, pp. 96-133).

Further, the sentence itself testifies to its general scope: "Ne autem tuus iste *gravis et perniciosus error* ac transgressio remaneat omnino impunitus, *et sis in exemplum aliis, ut abstineant ab hujusmodi delictis*." And so do the letters of publication: " Come vostra Reverenza," writes the Cardinal of S. Onofrio to the Inquisitor-General at Venice, "vedrà dall' allegata copia della sentenza ed abjura, che se le manda, *affinchè la notifichi a' suoi Vicari, e se ne abbia notizia da essi e da tutti i professori di filosofia e di matematica, perchè sapendo eglino in che modo si è trattato il detto Galileo, comprendano la gravità dell' errore da lui commesso, per evitarlo insieme con la pena, che, cadendovi, sarebbono per ricevere*."

"Atque hoc," writes the Nuncio Apostolic in Belgium to Jansenius, Rector of the University of Louvain, "Academiis Belgicis significari prædicta Sacra Congregatio voluit, *ut huic veritati se conformare omnes velint*. Ideo cæteros quoque ipsius Universitatis Professores a dominatione tua de hoc admoneri cupimus."[*]

Indisputably, then, the sentence of 1633 was a decision on a matter pertaining to doctrine put forth by a Pontifical Congregation ; and therefore, according to the Munich Brief, all Catholic men of science were bound to yield it intellectual submission.[†]

---

[*] *Opere*, vol. ix. p. 473.

[†] And that it was received by many as the voice of the Church, as a Pontifical decree, is certain. " An supradicta propositio," asks Polaccus, " quæ opinatur et tuetur terram mobilem esse, cœlos vero immobiles, sit hæretica, *maxime post abjurationem factam Romæ à Galileo*. . . . Sic modo *Ecclesia* se gessit, Sacræ Scripturæ loca, scilicet pro immobilitate terræ et cœlorum immobilitate, (*sic*) *quæ aliter absque hæresi adhuc a quibusdam interpretabantur, sua auctoritate ita confirmando, ut de illis amplius homini Christiano dubitare citra hæresim minime liceat* " (*Anticopernicus Catholicus*, pp. 64, 65).

" Vides," says the Jesuit Cazræus to Gassendi, " igitur quam ista periculose in publicum divulgentur, et a viris præsertim qui sua auctoritate fidem facere videantur ; et quam non immerito jam inde a Copernici tempore *Ecclesia* semper huic se errori opposuerit ; eumque etiam novissime non *Cardinales tantum aliqui, ut ais, sed supremum Ecclesiæ caput Pontificio decreto in Galileo damnaverit, et ut ne in posterum verbo aut scripto doceretur, sanctissime prohibuerit* " (quoted by Gassendi in his letter, " De Proportione qua gravia decedentia accelerantur " (Gassendi, *Opera*, tom. iii. p. 582).

I will now sum up the conclusions which the history of Galileo's case seems to me to teach in direct opposition to doctrine that has been authoritatively inculcated in Rome :—

1. Rome, *i.e.* a Pontifical Congregation acting under the Pope's order, may put forth a decision that is neither true nor safe.

"In argumento præsertim," remarks Scipio Claramontius in his *Antiphilolaus*, "et errore qui nedum philosophiæ, sed etiam pietati jam adversatur, geometricam et demonstrativam veritatem tribuit positioni ab *Ecclesia Pontificio decreto damnatæ*. Si vera est damnata positio, *sanctio quæ ut falsam damnat ipsa falsa erit*" (p. 8). And again : "Tertium caput propositorum restat, repugnare scilicet opinionem positionemque sacris literis, tantum abesse, ut illi faveant veluti dicebat Keplerus. Satis sane est Catholicis *decretum Sancta Ecclesia Catholicæ ad agnoscendam positionis falsitatem, cum edicto ipsa caverit ne quis amplius positioni Copernici tanquam veræ adhæreat*. Loca sunt in Sacra Scriptura quæ terram immobilem, cœlum mobile faciant, *quodque amplius est ex ejus interpretatione, cui vera sensa patent Scripturarum*. Spiritus enim prophetarum subditus est prophetis" (p. 187).

"Cur etenim et quarto," asks Morinus, "scribam contra telluris motum? Primo, quod D. Gassendus, vir inter hujusce temporis doctos valde celebris ac Ecclesiasticus, tali opinioni *ab Ecclesia quoque damnatæ* arma non pauca de novo subministrare est ausus. . . . Id autem præcipue debeo hac in causa pro qua jam ter scripsi, et mihi novo decreto sacrosancta favet Ecclesia."

"Profecto ipsi amicè consulo, ne cum sua fidei professione verbis satis ambiguis exposita, facie sit unquam Romipeta, sed semper Romifuga; vereor enim ne ibi durius tracteretur quam Galilæus" (Morinus, *Alæ. Telluris Fractæ*, pp. 1, 2, 7).

"Porro quam infaustis syderibus in lucem editus fuerit liber Galilæi, patet ex sententia adversus ipsum Romæ lata; quâ nimirum re ut par est examini commissa, doctrina de telluris motu dicitur in fide erronea et Scripturis contraria; liber Dialogorum Galilæi prohibetur, et Galilæus ipse ad publicam sui erroris abjurationem condemnatur. . . . Quod si hæreticis Galilæi condemnatio minus arriserit, saltem fateantur oportet, physicas omnes rationes, evidentissima S. Scripturæ testimonia et Sacrosanctæ Ecclesiæ Catholicæ decisiones, Spiritu Sancto Præside latas, et hic et in cæteris, eorum erroribus plane contrariari" (Morinus, *Responsio pro Telluris quiete*, p. 56).

And observe the tone Viviani, Galileo's disciple and enthusiastic admirer, found he must adopt in writing of the matter:

"Ma essendo già il Sig. Galileo, per l' altre sue ammirabili speculazioni, con immortal fama fino al cielo innalzato, e con tante novità acquistatosi tra gli uomini del divino, permesse l'Eterna Provvidenza ch' ei dimostrasse l' umanità sua con l' errare, mentre, nella discussione dei due Sistemi, si dimostrò più aderente all' ipotesi Copernicana, *già dannata da Santa Chiesa* come repugnante alla Divina Scriptura" (*Vita di Galileo da Viviani*).

On which Professor Albèri remarks, "Le parole che il Viviani si è qui creduto in obbligo di usare, parlando della condanna di Galileo, valgono più di un lungo ragionamento a rappresentarci la condizione dei tempi in cui quel fatto si consumava" (*Opere di G. G.* vol. xv. p. 352).

2. Decrees confirmed by, and virtually included in, a Bull addressed to the Universal Church, may be, not only scientifically false, but, theologically considered, dangerous, *i.e.* calculated to prejudice the cause of religion, and compromise the safety of a portion of the deposit committed to the Church's keeping. In other words, the Pope, in and by a Bull addressed to the whole Church, may confirm and approve, with Apostolic authority, decisions that are false and perilous to the faith.

3. Decrees of the Apostolic See and of Pontifical Congregations may be calculated to impede the free progress of science.*

4. The Pope's infallibility is no guarantee that he may not use his supreme authority to indoctrinate the Church with erroneous opinions, through the medium of Congregations he has erected to assist him in protecting the Church from error.

5. The Pope, through the medium of a Pontifical Congregation, may require, under pain of excommunication, individual Catholics to yield an absolute assent to false, unsound, and dangerous propositions. In other words, the Pope, acting as Supreme Judge of the faithful, may, in dealing with individuals, make the rejection of what is in fact the truth, a condition of communion with the Holy See.

6. It does not follow, from the Church's having been informed that the Pope has ordered a Catholic to abjure an opinion as a heresy, that the opinion is not true and sound.

7. The true interpretation of our Lord's promises to St. Peter permits us to say that a Pope may, even when acting officially, confirm his brethren the Cardinals,† and

---

* "Apostolicæ Sedis Romanorumque Congregationum decreta liberum scientiæ progressum impediunt" is one of the condemned errors in the Syllabus published by order of Pius IX.

† "Qui tanquam Sanctæ R. Ecclesiæ nobilissima membra capiti proprius cohærentia, eidem Summo Pontifici, sicut Christo Domino Apostoli, semper assistunt, quique primi laborum et consiliorum socii sunt et participes" ("Immensa æterni Dei," Cher. Bull. vol. ii. p. 667). "Qui vere sunt sal terræ ac lucernæ positæ super candelabrum, ut inter sanguinem et sanguinem, causam et causam, lepram et lepram discernant, ac doctrinæ opportunitate et

through them the rest of the Church, in an error as to
what is matter of faith.

8. It is not always for the good of the Church that
Catholics should submit themselves fully, perfectly, and
absolutely, *i.e.* should yield a full assent, to the decisions
of Pontifical Congregations, even when the Pope has confirmed such decisions with his supreme authority, and
ordered them to be published.

Are not all these propositions irreconcilable with
Ultramontane principles? If so, can it be denied that
those principles are as false as it is true that the earth
moves?

---

veritate, infirma confirment, disrupta consolident, depravata convertant,
luceant omnibus qui in domo Domini habitant, ac primæ huic Sedi assistentes
cunctos pastores, dum in gravioribus negotiis eandem Sedem consulunt,
ejusve opem implorant, suo judicio, consilio et auctoritate instruere, dirigere,
ac docere, non cessent" ("Postquam verus," Bull. vol. ii. p. 609).

"Eorum autem," says Fagnanus, "decisioni necessario parendum esse
aperte ostendunt subsequentia verba, *et facies quæcunque dixerint sequerisque
eorum sententiam*, &c. Hinc Cardinalis Paleot. *de Sacri Consistorii Consult.*
pars v. q. 40, dixit Congregationes Cardinalium quas Summi Pontifices et præsertim Sixtus V. ad causarum difficultates ipsius auctoritate cognoscendas et
definiendas instituerint, esse tanquam filias Consistorii ab eo veluti fonte per-
manentes. Et quemadmodum sol non solum ipse lucet, verum etiam stellis
lumen impertitur, quo et cœlum ornant et illuminant orbem universum, sic
Summum Pontificem, non suis decretis modo Ecclesiam per seipsum docere et
moderari, verum etiam ita Cardinales sua tum auctoritate fulcire, tum potes-
tate augere, ut sociatis laboribus facile omnes difficultatum nodos dissolvant"
(*Const. c. Quoniam*, tom. i. p. 132).

APPENDIX A.

Bellarmine's Letter to Father Foscarini, published by Professor Dom. Berti in his work, " Copernico e le vicende del Sistema Copernicano in Italia nella seconda metà del Secolo XVI. e nella prima del Secolo XVI. Roma, 1876."

MULTO R. Padre mio,

Ho letto volentieri l' epistola Italiana, e la scrittura latina che la P. V. mi ha mandato, la ringrazio dell' una e dell' altra, e confesso che sono tutte piene d' ingegno et di doctrina. Ma perchè lei dimanda il mio parere lo farò con multa brevità, perchè lei già ha poco tempo di leggere e io ho poco tempo di scrivere.

1. Dico che mi pare che V. P. et il Sig. Galileo facciano prudentemente a contentarsi di parlare ex suppositione e non assolutamente come io ho sempre creduto che abbia parlato il Copernico, perchè il dire che supposto che la terra si muove et il sole stia fermo si salvano tutte le apparenze meglio che con porre gli eccentrici et epicicli, è benissimo detto, e non ha pericolo nessuno, e questo basta al mathematico. Ma volere affermare, che realmente il sole stia nel centro del mondo, e sole si rivolti in se stesso senza correre dall' oriente all occidente, e che la terra stia nel 3 cielo e gira con somma velocita intorno al sole, è cosa molto pericolosa non solo d' irritare tutti i filosofi, e theologi scholastici, ma anco di nuocere alla santa fede con rendere false le Scritture Sante. Perchè la P. V. ha bene dimonstrato molti modi di esporre le Sante Scritture, ma non li ha applicati in particolare, che senza dubbio havria trovato grandissime difficoltà, se havesse voluto esporre tutti quei luoghi che lei stessa ha citato.

2. Dico che, come lei sa, il Concilio proibisce esporre le Scritture contra il commune consenso de' Santi Padri, e se la P. V. vorrà leggere, non dico solo li Santi Padri,

I

ma li commentarii moderni sopra il Genesi, sopra li Salmi, sopra l' Eclesiaste, sopra Giosuè, troverà che tutti convengono in esporre ad literam ch' il sole è nel cielo, e gira intorno alla terra con somma velocità, e che la terra è lontanissima dal cielo e sta nel centro del mondo immobile. Considera hora lei con la sua prudenza se la chiesa possa sopportare, che si dia alle Scritture un senso contrario alli Santi Padri, et a tutti li espositori greci e latini.

Nè si può rispondere che questa non sia materia di fede, perchè se non è materia di fede ex parte objecti, è materia di fede ex parte dicentis; e così sarebbe heretico chi dicesse che Abramo non abbia avuto due figliuoli, e Jacob dodici, come chi dicesse che Cristo non è nato di Vergine, perchè l' uno e l' altro lo dice lo Spirito Santo per bocca de' Profeti et Apostoli.

8. Dico, che quando ci fosse vera demostratione che il sole stia nel centro del mondo, e la terra nel 8 cielo, e che il sole non circonda la terra, ma la terra circonda il sole, allora bisogneria andar con molta consideratione in esplicare le Scritture che paiono contrarie, e più sotto dire che non l' intendiamo, che dire che sia falso quello che si dimostra. Ma io non crederò che ci sia tale dimostratione fin che non mi sia mostrata; nè è l' istesso dimostrare che supposto ch' il sole stia nel centro e la terra nel cielo si salvino le apparenze, e dimostrare che in verità il sole stia nel centro e la terra nel cielo. Perchè la prima dimostratione, credo che ci possa essere, ma della seconda ho grandissimo dubbio, e in caso di dubbio non si deve lasciare la Scrittura Santa esposta da Santi Padri. Aggiungo che quello che scrisse : " Oritur sol et occidit et ad locum suum revertitur," fu Salomone, il quale non solo parlò ispirato da Dio, ma fu huomo sopra tutti gli altri sapientissimo e dottissimo nelle scienze humane e nella cognitione delle cose create, et tutta questa sapienza l' hebbe da Dio ; onde non è verosimile che affermasse una cosa, che fosse contraria alla verità dimostrata, o che si potesse dimostrare. E se mi dirà che Salomone parla seconda l' apparenza, parendo a noi ·che il sole giri, mentre la terra gira, come a chi si parte dal litto, pare che il litto si parta della nave. Risponderò che chi si parte dal litto, se bene

gli pare che il litto si parta da lui, nondimeno conosce che questo è errore, e lo corregge, vedendo chiaramente che la nave si muove, e non il litto. Ma quanto al sole e la terra, nessuno savio è che habbia bisogno di correggere l' errore, perchè chiaramente experimenta che la terra stà firma, e che l' occhio non s' inganna quando giudica che il sole si muove, come anco non s' inganna quando giudica che la luna, e le stelle, si muovano; e questo basti per hora. Con che saluto caramente V. P. gli prego da Dio ogni contento.

Di casa. Li. 12 di Aprile 1615, di V. P. M. R. come fratello il Car. Bellarmino.

APPENDIX B.

Extracts from the Vatican MS. minutes, published by M. Henri de l'Epinois in his work, " Les Pièces du Procès de Galilée," pp. 38, 41.

F. 375 v°.:

Die 25 Novembris 1615 videantur quædam litteræ Gallilei editæ Romæ cum inscriptione " delle macchie solari."

F. 376 r°. :

Propositio censuranda :

Che il sole sii centro del mondo et per conseguenza immobile di moto locale :

Che la terra non è centro del mondo nè immobile, ma si muove secondo se tutta etiam di moto diurno.

Erit congregatio qualificationis in S. Officio, die Martis 23 Februarii, hora decimaquarta cum dimidia.

F. 376 v°.:

Die 19 Februarii 1616, fuit missa copia omnibus RR. PP. DD. Theologis.

F. 377 r°. :

Censura facta in S. Officio Urbis, die Mercurii 24 Februarii 1616, coram infrascriptis patribus theologis.

Propositiones censurandæ.

Prima : Sol est centrum mundi et omnino immobilis motu locali.

Censura: Omnes dixerunt dictam propositionem esse stultam et absurdam in philosophia et formaliter hereticam, quatenus contradicit expresse sententiis Sacræ Scripturæ in multis locis secundum proprietatem verborum et secundum communem expositionem et sensum Sanctorum Patrum et Theologorum Doctorum.

Secunda: Terra non est centrum mundi nec immobilis, sed secundum se totam movetur, etiam motu diurno.

Censura: Omnes dixerunt hanc propositionem recipere eandum censuram in philosophia et spectando veritatem theologicam ad minus esse in fide erroneam.

Petrus Lombardus, Archiepiscopus Armacanus.

Fr. Hyacintus Petronius, Sacri Apostolici palatii magister.

Fr. Raphael Riphoz, theologiæ magister et vicarius generalis Ordinis Prædicatorum.

Fr. Michael Angelus, Seg. Sacræ theologiæ magister et Commissarius S. Officii.

Fr. Hieronimus de Casali Majori, Consultor S. Officii.

Fr. Thomas de Lemos.

Fr. Gregorius Nunnius Coronel.

Benedictus Justinianus (?), Societatis Jesu.

D. Raphael Rastellius, clerus regularis, doctor theologus.

D. Michael a Neapoli, ex Congregatione Cassinensi.

Fr. Jacobus Tintus, socius Rmi. Patris Commissarii S. Officii.

F. 378 v°.:

Die Jovis 25 Februarii 1616 Illmus. D. Cardinalis Millinus notificavit RR. PP. DD. Assessori et Commissario S. Officii, quod relata censura PP. theologorum ad propositiones Gallilei mathematici quod sol sit centrum mundi et immobilis motu locali, et terra moveatur etiam motu diurno, Smus. ordinavit Illmo. D. Cardinali Bellarmino ut vocet coram se dictum Galileum, eumque moneat ad deserendam dictam opinionem; et si recusaverit parere, P. Commissarius coram Notario et testibus faciat illi præceptum ut omnino abstineat hujusmodi doctrinam et opinionem docere, aut defendere, seu de ea tractare; si vero non acquieverit, carceretur.

Die Veneris 26 ejusdem.

In palatio solitæ habitationis dicti Illmi. Cardinalis Bellarmini et in mansionibus Dominationis suæ Illmæ. idem Illmus. D. Cardinalis vocato supradicto Galileo, ipsoque coram D. S. Illma. existente, in presentia admodum R. P. fratris Michaelis Angeli Seghitii de Lauda, Ordinis Prædicatorum, commissarii generalis S. Officii, predictum Galileum monuit de errore supradictæ opinionis et ut illam deserat; et successive ac incontinenti in mei, &, et testium &, presente etiam adhuc eodem Illmo. D. Cardinali, supradictus P. Commissarius predicto Galileo adhuc ibidem presenti et constituto precepit et ordinavit, (proprio nomine *) Smi. D. N. Papæ (f. 379 rº.) et totius Congregationis S. Officii, ut supradictam opinionem quod sol sit centrum mundi et immobilis et terra moveatur omnino relinquat, nec eam de cætero, quovis modo teneat, doceat, aut defendat, verbo aut scriptis, alias contra ipsum procedetur in S. Officio; cui precepto idem Galileus acquievit et parere promisit, super quibus, &c. . . . actum Romæ ubi supra; presentibus ibidem R. D. Badino Nores de Nicosia in regno Cypri, et Augustino Mongardo de loco abbatiæ Rosæ, diocesis Politianensis, familiaribus dicti Illmi. D. Cardinalis, testibus.

Feria v. die iii. Martii 1616.

Facta relatione per Illumum. D. Card. Bellarminum quod Galilæus Galilei mathematicus monitus de ordine Sacræ Congregationis ad deserendam opinionem quam hactenus tenuit quod sol sit centrum spherarum, et immobilis, terra autem mobilis, acquievit; ac relato Decreto Congregationis Indicis, qualiter (o, variante, quod) fuerunt prohibita et suspensa respective scripta Nicolai Copernici (De revolutionibus orbium cœlestium) Didaci a Stunica in Job, et Fr. Pauli Antonii Foscarini Carmelitæ, SSmus. ordinavit publicari Edictum a P. Magistro S. Palatii hujusmodi suspensionis et prohibitionis respective.†

* See facsimile of MS. in *Les Pièces du Procès*, and M. de l'Epinois' remark.

† Doc. vi. from the collection of documents published by Professor Silvestro Gherardi in the *Rivista Europea*, anno i. vol. iii. 1870.

APPENDIX C.

Bellarmine's Certificate.

Noi Roberto Cardinale Bellarmino havendo inteso che il Sig. Galileo Galilei sia calunniato, o imputato di havere abjurato in mano nostra, et anco di essere stato perciò penitenziato di penitenzie salutari; et essendo ricercati della verità, diciamo che il suddetto Sig. Galileo non ha abjurato in mano nostra, nè di altri qua in Roma, ne meno in altro luogo, che noi sappiamo, alcuna sua opinione o dottrina, ne manco ha ricevuto penitenzie salutari, nè d'altra sorte: ma solo gli è stata denunziata la dichiarazione fatta da Nostro Signore, et publicata dalla Sacra Congregatione dell' Indice, nella quale si contiene, che la dottrina attribuita al Copernico, che la terra si muova intorno al sole, e che il sole stia nel centro del mondo senza muoversi da oriente ad occidente, sia contraria alle Sacre Scritture, et pero non si possa difendere, ne tenere. E in fede di ciò habbiamo scritta e sottoscritta la presente di nostra propria mano: questo dì 26 di Maggio 1616.

Il medesimo di sopra,

ROBERTO CARD. BELLARMINO.*

APPENDIX D.

Monitum Sacræ Congregationis ad Nicolai Copernici lectorem, ejusque emendatio, permissio, et correctio.

Quamquam scripta Nicolai Copernici, nobilis astrologi, de mundi revolutionibus prorsus prohibenda esse patres Sacræ Congregationis Indicis censuerunt, ea ratione, quia principia de situ et motu terreni globi Sacræ Scripturæ, ejusque veræ et catholicæ interpretationi repugnantia (quod in homine Christiano minime tolerandum est) non per hypothesim tractare, sed ut verissima adstruere non dubitat: nihilominus quia in iis multa sunt reipublicæ utilissima, unanimi consensu in eam iverunt sententiam,

* From Marini, *Galileo e l' Inquisizione*, pp. 101, 102, with M. de l'Epinois' ⁀ctions.

ut Copernici opera ad hanc usque diem impressa permittenda essent, prout permiserunt, iis tamen correctis, juxta subjectam emendationem, locis, in quibus non ex hypothesi sed asserendo de situ et motu terræ disputat. Qui vero deinceps imprimendi erunt, non nisi prædictis locis ut sequitur emendatis, et hujusmodi correctione præfixa Copernici præfationi, permittuntur.

Locorum, quæ in Copernici libris visa sunt correctione digna emendatio.

In præfatione circa finem.—Ibi *si fortasse* dele omnia, usque ad verba, *hi nostri labores;* et sic accommoda, *cæterum hi nostri labores.*

In capite i. libri i. p. 6.—Ibi *si tamen attentius,* corrige, *si tamen attentius rem consideremus, nihil refert terram in medio mundi, vel extra medium existere, quoad solvendas cœlestium motuum apparentias: omnis enim, &c.*

In capite viii. ejusdem libri.—Totum hoc caput posset expungi, quia ex professo tractat de veritate motus terræ, dum solvit veterum rationes probantes ejus quietem: cum tamen problematice semper videatur loqui, ut studiosis satisfiat, et series, et ordo libri integer maneat, emendetur ut infra.

Primo, p. 6, dele versiculum *cur ergo* usque ad verbum *provehimur,* locusque ita corrigatur: *Cur ergo non possumus mobilitatem illi formæ suæ concedere, magisque quod totus labatur mundus, cujus finis ignoratur, scirique nequit, et quæ apparent in cœlo, perinde se habere, ac si diceret Virgilianus Æneas, &c.*

Secundo, pag. 7, versiculus *addo* corrigatur in hunc modum: *addo etiam difficilius non esse contento et locato, quod est terra, motum ascribere, quam continenti.* Tertio, eadem pagina, in fine capitis, versiculus *vides,* delendus est usque ad finem capitis.

In capite ix. p. 7.—Principium hujus capitis usque ad versiculum *quod enim* ita corrige: *Cum igitur terram moveri assumpserim, videndum nunc arbitror, an etiam illi plures possint convenire motus, quod enim, &c.*

In capite x. p. 9.—Versiculum *proinde* corrige sic: *Proinde non pudet nos assumere.* Et paulo infra, ibi, *hoc potius in mobilitate terræ* verificari, corrige, hoc consequentur in mobilitate terræ verificari. Pagina 10, in fine capitis, dele illa verba postrema : *Tanta nimirum est divina hæc Dei optimi maximi fabrica.*

In capite xi.—Titulus capitis accommodetur hoc modo : *De hypothesi triplicis motus terræ, ejusque demonstratione.*

In libro iv. capite x. p. 122.—In titulo capitis dele verba, *horum trium siderum,* quia terra non est sidus, ut facit eam Copernicus.*

FRATER FRANCISCUS MAGDALENUS CAPIFERREUS,

Ordinis Prædicatorum, Sacræ Congregationis Secretarius.

Romæ, ex typographia Carm. Apos., 1620.

APPENDIX E.

The Decree of Urban VIII. of the 16th of June 1633, that Galileo, if he stood the threat of torture, was to be made to abjure de vehementi sub pœna relapsus, and the Pope's subsequent command to publish the sentence and abjuration, from the documents published by Professor Gherardi, in the " Rivista Europea," anno i. vol. iii., 1870.

XIII. Feria v. die xvi. Junii 1633.

Galilæi de Galileis Florentini, in hoc S. Off. carcerati et ob ejus adversam valetudinem ac senectutem cum præcepto de non discedendo de domo electæ habitationis in urbe, ac de se repræsentando toties quoties sub pœnis arbitrio Sacræ Congregationis habilitati, proposita causa, relato processu, et auditis votis, Smus. decrevit ipsum interrogandum esse super intentione et comminata ei tortura, et si sustinuerit, previa abjuratione de vehementi in plena Congregatione S. Off. condemnandum ad carcerem arbitrio Sac. Congregationis. Injunctum ei ne de cetero scripto vel verbo tractet amplius quovis modo de mobilitate terræ, nec de stabilitate solis et e contra, sub pœna relapsus. Librum vero ab eo conscriptum cui titulus est Dialogo di Galileo Galilei Linceo (publice cremandum fore (*sic*) ma cassato) prohibendum fore. Præterea ut hæc omnibus innotescant, exemplaria Sententiæ Decretumque

---

* This last correction does not appear in the Index of Alexander VII.

perinde transmitti jussit ad omnes Nuntios Apostolicos, et ad omnes hæreticæ pravitatis Inquisitores, ac præcipue ad Inquisitorem Florentiæ qui eam sententiam in ejus plena Congregatione, Consultoribus accersitis, etiam et coram plerisque Mathematicæ Artis Professoribus, publice legat.

XIV. Feria iv. die 22 Junii 1638.

Galilæus de Galilæis Florentin. abjuravit de vehementi in Congregatione &c., (sic) juxta formulam &c. (sic).

XVI. Feria v. die 30 Junii 1633.

SSmus. mandavit Inquisitori Florentiæ mitti copiam Sententiæ et Abjurationis Galilæi de Galilæis Florentini Professoris Philosophiæ et Mathematicæ, ut illam legi faciat coram Consultoribus et Officialibus S. Officii, vocatis etiam Professoribus Philosophiæ et Mathematicæ ejusdem civitatis in Congregatione S. O. velo levato (sic): eamdemque pariter copiam Sententiæ et Abjurationis mitti omnibus Nuntiis Apostolicis et Inquisitoribus locorum, et in primis Inquisitoribus Bononiæ et Paduæ, qui illam notificari mandent eorum Vicariis et Diocæsanis, ut deveniat ad notitiam omnino Professorum Philosoph. et Mathem.

APPENDIX F.

*The Sentence pronounced on Galileo by the Congregation of the Inquisition, and his Abjuration.**

SENTENZA.

Noi Gasparo del titolo di S. Croce in Gierusalemme Borgia.

Fra Felice Centino del titolo di S. Anastasia, detto d' Ascoli.

Guido del titolo di S. Maria del Popolo Bentivoglio.

Fra Desiderio Scaglia del titolo de S. Carlo, detto di Cremona.

* From the work of Giorgius Polaccus entitled " Anticopernicus Catholicus seu de terræ statione et de solis motu, contra systema Copernicanum Catholicæ assertionis " (Venice, 1644). The Italian texts of these documents are almost certainly the original. See Sousa, *Aphor. Inqui.* lib. ii. c. xl. p. 379; *Sacra Arsenale*, pp. 353-4, xlix.; Carena, *De Off. S. Inq.* pars iii. tit. xii. 31.

Fra Antonio Barberino, detto di S. Onofrio.

Laudivio Zacchia del titolo di S. Pietro in Vincola, detto di S. Sisto.

Berlingero del titolo di S. Agustino, Gessi.

Fabricio del titolo di S. Lorenzo in pane, e perna.

Verospi, chiamato Prete.

Francesco di S. Lorenzo in Damaso Barbarino, e

Martio di S. Maria Nuova Ginetti Diaconi,

Per la misericordia di Dio della S.R.E. Cardinali in tutta la republica Christiana contra l' eretica pravità Inquisitori Generali della S. Sede Apostolica specialmente deputati.

Essendo che tu Galileo figliolo del qu. Vincenzo Galilei Fiorentino del età tua d' anni 70 fosti denonciato del 1615 in questo S. Officio, che tenessi come vera la falsa dottrina da molti insegnata, che il Sole sia centro del mondo et immobile, e che la terra si muova anco di moto diurno : Che avevi alcuni discepoli, a' quali insegnavi la medesima doctrina : Che circa l' istessa tenevi corrispondenza con alcuni Matematici di Germania : Che tu avevi dato alle stampe alcune lettere intitolate delle Macchie Solari, nelle quali spiegavi l' istessa doctrina, come vera : Et che all' obbiezioni, chi alle volte ti venivano fatte tolte della Sacra Scriptura rispondevi glossando detta Scrittura conforme al tuo senso. E successivamente fu presentata copia d' una scrittura sotto forma di lettera, quale si diceva essere stata scritta da te ad un tale già tuo discepolo, ed in essa seguendo la posizione di Copernico, si contengono varie proposizioni contro il vero senso, ed autorità della sacra Scrittura.

Volendo per ciò questo S. Tribunale provvedere al disordine ed al danno, che di quì proveniva, et andava crescendosi con pregiudizio della Santa Fede ; d' ordine di Nostro Signore, e degli Emin. Signori Cardinali di questa suprema et universale Inquisizione, furono dalli Qualificatori Teologi qualificate le due proposizioni della stabilità del Sole, e del moto della terra ; cioè,

Che il Sole sia centro del mondo, et immobile di moto locale, è proposizione assurda e falsa in filosofia, e formal-

mente eretica, per essere espressamente contraria alla
sacra Scrittura.

Che la terra non sia centro del mondo, nè immobile,
ma che si move etiandio di moto diurno, è parimenti
proposizione assurda e falsa nella filosofia, e considerata
in teologia, ad minus erronea in fide.

Ma volendosi per allora proceder teco con benignità, fu
decretato nella S. Congregazione tenuta avanti Nostro
Signore à 25 Febbraro 1616, che l' Eminentissimo Signor
Cardinale Bellarmino ti ordinasse che tu dovessi onninamente lasciare la detta dottrina falsa, e ricusando tu di
ciò fare, che dal commissario del S. Uffizio ti dovesse
esser fatto precetto di lasciar la detta dottrina, e che
non potessi insegnarla ad altri, nè difenderla, nè trattarne;
al qual precetto non acquietandoti, dovessi esser carce-
rato; et in esecuzione dell' istesso decreto, il giorno
sequente nel Palazzo, et alla presenza del suddetto
Eminentissimo Signore Cardinale Bellarmino, dopo essere
stato dall istesso Signor Cardinale benignamente avvisato
et ammonito, ti fu dal P. Commissario del S. Uffizio di
quel tempo fatto precetto, con notaro e testimonii, che
onninamente dovessi lasciar la detta falsa opinione, e che
nell' avenire tu non la potessi, nè defendere, nè insegnare
in qual si voglia modo, nè in voce, nè in scritto; et
avendo tu promesso d' obbedire, fosti licenziato.

Et acciocchè si togliesse affatto così perniciosa dottrina, e non andasse più oltre serpendo, in grave pregiudizio della cattolica verità, uscì decreto della sacra Congregazione dell' Indice, col quale furono proibiti i libri,
che trattano di tal dottrina, et essa dichiarata falsa, et
onninamente contraria alla sacra e divina Scrittura.

Et essendo ultimamente comparso quà un libro stam-
pato in Fiorenza l' anno prossimo passato, la cui inscrizione
mostra che tu ne fossi l' autore, dicendo il titolo : *Dialogo di
Galileo Galilei delli due massimi sistemi del Mondo, Tolemaico
e Copernicano;* et informata appresso la sacra Congregazione, che con l' impressione di detto libro ogni giorno più
prendeva piede la falsa opinione del moto della terra e
stabilità del Sole; fu il detto libro diligentemente con-
siderato, e in esso trovata apertamente la transgressione

del suddetto precetto che ti fu fatto, avendo tu nel medesimo libro difesa la detta opinione già dannata, et in faccia tua per tale dichiarata, avvenga che tu in detto libro con varii raggiri ti studii di persuadere, che tu la lasci, come indecisa et espressamente probabile. Il che pure è errore gravissimo, non potendo in modo niuno esser probabile un' opinione dichiarata e difinita per contraria alla Scrittura divina.

Che perciò d' ordine nostro fosti chiamato a questo S. Uffizio, nel quale con tuo giuramento esaminato riconoscesti il libro come da te composto, e dato alle stampe. Confessasti, che dieci, o dodici anni sono in circa, dopo essersi fatto il precetto come sopra, cominciasti a scrivere detto libro. Che chiedesti la facoltà di stamparlo, senza però significare a quelli che ti diedero simile facoltà, che tu avessi precetto di non tenere, defendere, nè insegnare in qualsivoglia modo tal dottrina.

Confessasti parimenti che la scrittura di detto libro è in più luoghi distesa in tal forma, che il lettore potrebbe formar concetto, che gli argomenti portati per la parte falsa fossero in tal giusa pronunciati, che più tosto per la loro efficacia fossero potenti a stringere, che facili ad esser sciolti; scusandoti d' esser incorso in error tanto alieno, come dicesti, della tua intenzione, per aver scritto in Dialogo, e per la natural compiacenza, che ciascheduno ha delle proprie sottigliezze, e del mostrarsi più arguto del commune degli uomini, in trovar, anco per le proposizioni false, ingegnosi et apparenti discorsi di probabilità.

Et essendoti stato assegnato termine conveniente a far le tue difese, producesti una fede scritta di mano dell' Eminentissimo Signor Cardinale Bellarmino da te procurata come dicesti, per defenderti dalle calunnie de' tuoi nemici, da' quali ti veniva opposto, che avevi abjurato, e fossi stato penitenziato dal Santo Offizio. Nella qual fede si dice, che tu non avevi abjurato, nè meno eri stato penitenziato, ma che ti era solo stata denunciata la dichiarazione fatta da Nostro Signore e publicata dalla santa

Lightning Source UK Ltd.
Milton Keynes UK
UKHW022058160223
417160UK00003B/230

9 781019 079201